Post-Conflict Reconstruction
The Role of the World Bank

The World Bank
Washington, D.C.

The main text of this volume was endorsed by the Board of Directors
of the World Bank in May 1997 under the title "A Framework for
World Bank Involvement in Post-Conflict Reconstruction." Statistics
and titles of Bank departments have been updated, but otherwise the
text remains the same as in the original Board document. Annex C,
"World Bank Operational Guidelines for Financing Landmine Clearance" was prepared by the Operations Policy Department of the
World Bank and distributed to staff in February 1997.

Cover photograph: Beirut, Lebanon. Curt Carnemark.

Library of Congress Cataloging-in-Publication Data

Post-conflict reconstruction : the role of the World Bank.
    p. cm.
  Includes bibliographical references.
  ISBN 0-8213-4215-0
  1. World Bank. 2. Economic assistance—Developing countries.
I. World Bank. Environmentally and Socially Sustainable
Development Network.
HG3881.5.W57P67   1998
658.1'532—dc21   98-17913
                                                       CIP

Contents

Annexes

Boxes

Foreword

The sustainable reconstruction of countries emerging from long periods of conflict is a challenge we ignore at our peril. Since 1980, nearly half of all low-income countries have experienced major conflict. During the past 10 years, practically every country in Africa has either experienced major conflict or borders on another country that has experienced conflict. More recently we have seen conflict bring relatively prosperous societies such as the former Yugoslavia into poverty. This is not an issue we can relegate to the sidelines of development.

Significant portions of the resources of the International Development Association, the concessional window for World Bank lending, have been allocated to countries emerging from conflict. We have also increased our capacity to contribute to international efforts to deal with specific aspects of post-conflict reconstruction, such as the demobilization and reintegration of ex-combatants and refugees. The Bank has also begun programs to help address the issue of land mine clearance, which blocks reconstruction and development in many post-conflict countries. At the request of international donors, our institution has played a key role in coordinating international aid in Bosnia and Herzegovina and the West Bank and Gaza and other transitional situations through the Holst Fund and other mechanisms. In addition, in cases of urgent need, the Board of Governors of the Bank has approved ad hoc grants in specific situations to facilitate the international effort. In the past five years, nearly $400 million in grants from the surplus of the Bank have been given to post-conflict governments and to the humanitarian efforts of our sister United Nations agencies to ameliorate the human suffering associated with conflict and to jump-start reconstruction efforts.

This report tries to bring those activities together and articulate a role for the Bank as a key actor in supporting the transition of countries involved in conflict into periods of sustainable peace. The framework that it outlines draws on the best practice of our operations to date, sketches out guidelines for Bank staff, and details some of the specific actions that will be taken to help the institution respond in this area. It focuses on the comparative advantage of the World Bank, as a development organization, in supporting specific aspects of this transition and emphasizes the critical importance of a worldwide partnership among the Bank, the United Nations system, the International Monetary Fund, and other international institutions in achieving progress in this vital undertaking.

Within this framework, in addition to addressing the concerns of post-conflict reconstruction, the Bank and its partners must begin to ask hard questions about how we can best integrate a concern for conflict prevention into development operations. While our Articles of Agreement prohibit us from intervening in the domestic political affairs of our clients, the framework emphasizes that the Bank must take steps to ensure that the activities it supports "do no harm" and avoid aggravating existing inequities in fragile situations. We must also support member governments' attempts to ameliorate the conditions that may lead to conflict, through distributive policies and the participation of excluded groups in development. In that regard, you will find that much of the discussion in this report is intimately interrelated with other Bank initiatives in combating corruption and expanding our work on governance, social inclusion, and social capital.

During the first year of operation under this new framework, the World Bank has made important progress in increasing its capacity to respond in this area. We have created a new Post-Conflict Unit to help focus our efforts and concentrate scarce skills on the transition from war to peace. We are extremely grateful to many of our bilateral partners who have seconded staff to the new unit to allow it to represent a truly hybrid mix of talent and experience. Last summer we instituted a new grant facility, the Post-Conflict Fund, as part of our Development Grant Facility to begin to reinforce our capacity to respond early to reconstruction situations, and we have expanded our efforts to promote partnership with a wide range of agencies that share our concerns, especially the United Nations High Commissioner for Refugees, the United Nations Children's Fund, and the International Committee of the Red Cross. It is also essential that we develop strong and constructive relationships with civil society and the private sector. Along with development institutions and the governments concerned, they play a vital role in the reconstruction process.

The way ahead is not always certain. Development institutions cannot resolve conflicts. But the transition by societies from conflict to a consolidated peace can be supported by a series of well-timed technical interventions that remove some of the core impediments to post-conflict reconstruction and build a firmer base for socially sustainable development. In the end, the rationale for Bank action is a simple one: we will not have peace without economic hope. We must approach the challenge with humility and constant review. This report should be seen as the beginning of a dialogue. It is, I feel, a good beginning, which provides us with a solid base for action. I hope you will read it and get back to us with your comments.

James D. Wolfensohn
President
The World Bank

Acknowledgments

This report was prepared by a team composed of Steven Holtzman, Ann Elwan, and Colin Scott. The process began under the guidance of Armeane Choksi and Ishrat Husain and continued with the support and encouragement of Ismail Serageldin, Andrew Steer, and Gloria Davis. We are particularly grateful to Ishrat Husain for his advice and inputs in the early stages of the drafting process.

In many ways, this report is far more than the work of a group of individuals. It is the result of significant contributions by a wide range of Bank staff and managers who provided their time and shared the distillation of their long experience. There is not adequate space to allow us to mention by name all those others who made key contributions to this process. But some specific contributions deserve mention. Caio K. Koch-Weser and Ibrahim Shihata had substantial input into the final version. Mark Malloch Brown, Andreas Rigo, John D. Shilling, and Mohan Gopal were all generous with their advice. Many of the recommendations of the framework stem directly from extensive comments provided by Christine Wallich and Nigel Roberts on their experiences in helping to set up two seminal Bank programs in this area, respectively, in Bosnia and Herzegovina and in the West Bank and Gaza. Nigel kindly prepared the box on the West Bank and Gaza. Nat Colletta provided a box on the Bank's experience with demobilization and reintegration of ex-combatants in Uganda and otherwise shared his substantial expertise. Thanks to Julian Blackwood for sharing his experience on IGPRA and Paolo Caputo for developing the box.

Others who provided detailed comment at various stages of the many drafts include Robert Picciotto, Carolyn Jungr, Mary Sheehan, John Eriksson, Ian Bannon, Nils Tcheyan, Mamadou Dia, Borje Tallroth, Susan Rutledge, and Peter Miovic. Annex C, Bank operational guidelines on demining was drafted largely by Samir Bhatia, Steven Holtzman, and Mohan Gopal under the guidance of Myrna Alexander. We also wish to thank the wide range of colleagues from UN agencies, bilateral donors, nongovenmental organizations and others who reviewed various drafts and gave their comments and advice. Special thanks go to Anju

Sachdeva for patiently preparing dozens of drafts and sitting through this process. A note of gratitude should be offered to all those Executive Directors of the World Bank and their staff who worked closely with us over two years to finalize this report and put it into print.

Summary

The World Bank Group was established to support the reconstruction of Europe following World War II.[1] Fifty years later, the nature, scale, and proliferation of conflicts (particularly intrastate conflicts) in the post–cold war era are undermining development in a wide range of countries, threatening national and regional stability in some areas and diverting international attention and scarce resources from pressing development problems. In recent years operations in countries emerging from conflict have become a significant proportion of the Bank's portfolio. Excluding India and China, nearly a quarter of commitments by the International Development Association (IDA) are going to countries that have undergone or are emerging from intrastate conflict.

Although significant experience is developing in this area, a great deal remains to be learned. Much of the Bank's work in post-conflict reconstruction has been in rebuilding infrastructure—a traditional area of strength—but recent operations suggest this is not enough. There is a need for capacity to promote economic adjustment and recovery, to address social sector needs, and to build institutional capacity. New lending operations also involve unique post-conflict elements, including demining, demobilization and reintegration of ex-combatants, and reintegration of displaced populations. The activities supported by the Bank during this period are increasingly part of a comprehensive and interrelated package of interventions designed to facilitate the transition from conflict to peace.

To date the Bank has responded flexibly to this challenge. However, up-front costs (in terms of the staff time and senior management attention necessary to remove constraints and enable operations to proceed in a timely fashion) have been high. Experience in Bosnia and Herzegovina and the West Bank and Gaza, for example, illustrates the critical value of early planning and preparation for reconstruction programs. Often Bank operations have closed in countries in which the impact of conflict has made normal development activities impossible.

---

[1] The World Bank Group consists of the International Bank for Reconstruction and Development (IBRD) and its affiliates: the International Development Association (IDA), the International Finance Corporation (IFC), the Multilateral Investment Guarantee Agency (MIGA), and the International Centre for Settlement of Investment Disputes (ICSID).

The lack of clearly defined guidelines has complicated the ability of the Bank to plan efficiently a phased return to post-conflict countries.

The purpose of this report is to provide a conceptual and operational framework for Bank staff working in post-conflict situations, while encouraging the ingenuity, creativity, and initiative appropriate to individual country situations. The recommendations for change consolidate much of what has already been learned, rather than leading the Bank into new territory. The overall development of this new framework has taken place in the context of widespread consultation with operational staff in concerned countries and has benefited from significant consultation with the Bank's Executive Directors and senior management and with a broad circle of international actors—the United Nations agencies, nongovernmental organizations (NGOs), and representatives of concerned governments.

The Impact of Conflict

Both the extent of conflict worldwide and the impact of modern intrastate conflicts necessitate new strategies and modalities for post-conflict reconstruction. More than 50 countries have experienced significant periods of conflict since 1980, often resulting in a complete breakdown of the state. The proportion of official development assistance devoted to relief increased from 2 percent in 1989 to 10 percent in 1994, and peacekeeping operations alone cost the international community $3 billion in 1995.[2] Although conflict has touched both rich and poor societies, its effect on low-income countries has been most severe. Fifteen of the 20 poorest countries in the world have had a major conflict in the past 15 years. Conflicts have spilled across borders affecting neighboring states. Nearly every low-income country is adjacent to a country that has experienced breakdown and war.

Most recent conflicts have been intrastate conflicts. The transition to peace is often characterized by insecurity, uncertainty, and repeated cycles of violence before lasting solutions take hold. Thirty countries have had more than 10 percent of their population displaced through conflict; in 10 countries the proportion is more than 40 percent. More than 90 percent of the casualties have been civilians. More than 100 million land mines have been laid, causing casualties and blocking economic development long after the guns are silent. Whole generations have grown up in cultures of armed warfare and violence. Conflict has impoverished countries in every major region, in many cases wiping out the achievements of decades of economic and social development. Intrastate

---

[2] Dollar amounts are current U.S. dollars.

wars have been particularly damaging in Africa, directly or indirectly touching virtually every country. The destruction of physical assets, disruption in trade links, and loss of human capital are devastating but are only part of the problem. Violent conflict also leaves a legacy of militarized and divided societies, widespread displacement, and decimated institutional capacity.

The World Bank and other development institutions need a better understanding of the nature of violent conflict and of the accompanying social and economic disintegration. Many recent conflicts have had a base in ethnic or religious competition. But the underlying factors beneath these manifestations are more complex and impinge upon economic, social, and political relationships. Other conflicts are linked to competition for scarce resources. Often, conflict situations that might otherwise subside are fanned into conflagration by the actions of external actors or local political entrepreneurs. No conflict explodes due to one of these variables alone, but invariably occurs through a sequence of events.

In any given situation there are opportunities for external actors to affect the shape of events. Given the complexity of conflict, it may be unrealistic to expect development agencies to prevent conflicts from occurring, but it is important to integrate a sensitivity to conflict into the vision of development. The Bank has a significant role to play in developing such an expanded vision. Steps should be taken to ensure that interventions by development agencies do not aggravate existing inequities. The Bank, along with other development agencies, should support efforts by member governments to promote activities that ameliorate conditions which could lead to conflict. In the normal course of Bank operations, social assessments can help to identify fault lines of social tension and unequal patterns of distribution of resources within a society that may, in combination with other factors, fuel conflict. Engagement with civil society can contribute to a better understanding of how conflicts can be prevented. Increased focus on investments in good governance, incorporating elements of accountability, and transparency is also important.

The Bank's Role in Post-Conflict Reconstruction

In formulating its framework for supporting transitions from conflict, the Bank is guided by the following principles. The Bank is an international organization with a mandate, defined in its Articles of Agreement, to finance and facilitate reconstruction and development in its member countries. The Bank is not in charge of peacemaking or peacekeeping. It is not a governmental body for borrowing countries. These are functions of the United Nations and certain regional organizations. Under the explicit provisions of its Articles of Agreement, the Bank does not question the political character of a member and should not interfere in the domestic political affairs of a member. The Bank does not operate in the territory of a member without the approval of that member. Finally, the Bank is not a relief agency.

Post-conflict reconstruction begins by supporting the transition from conflict to peace in an affected country through the rebuilding of the country's socioeconomic framework. Given the nature of intrastate conflict, the formal cessation of hostilities does not necessarily signify that the process of transition is complete, although it does represent a critical point along this path. Reconstruction does not refer only to the reconstruction of "physical infrastructure," nor does it necessarily signify a rebuilding of the socioeconomic framework that existed before the onset of conflict. Conflict, particularly if it goes on for a long time, transforms a society, and a return to the past may not be possible or desirable. What is needed is the reconstruction of the *enabling conditions* for a functioning peacetime society. The role of external agencies, including the World Bank, is not to implement this process but, rather, to support it.

Post-conflict reconstruction has two overall objectives: to facilitate the transition to sustainable peace after hostilities have ceased and to support economic and social development. Economic recovery depends on the success of this transition and on the rebuilding of the domestic economy and restoration of access to external resources. These objectives imply an integrated package of reconstruction assistance to:

- Jump-start the economy through investment in key productive sectors; create the conditions for resumption of trade, savings, and domestic and foreign investment; and promote macroeconomic stabilization, rehabilitation of financial institutions, and restoration of appropriate legal and regulatory frameworks
- Reestablish the framework of governance by strengthening government institutions, restoring law and order, and enabling the organizations of civil society to work effectively
- Repair important physical infrastructure, including key transport, communication, and utility networks
- Rebuild and maintain key social infrastructure; that is, financing education and health, including recurrent costs
- Target assistance to those affected by war through reintegration of displaced populations, demobilization and reintegration of ex-combatants, revitalization of the local communities most disrupted by conflict through such means as credit lines to subsistence agri-

culture and microenterprises, and support for vulnerable groups
such as female-headed households

- Support land mine action programs, where relevant, including mine
surveys and demining of key infrastructure, as part of comprehensive development strategies for supporting a return to normal life
of populations living in mine-polluted areas
- Normalize financial borrowing arrangements by planning a workout of arrears, debt rescheduling, and the longer-term path to financial normalization.

Working conditions in post-conflict countries, with their limited government capacity, fragile political balances, and extreme time pressures, exacerbate the risks of reversals, setbacks, and failures. The risks of doing business are much higher than in "normal" developing countries. They include (a) risks related to "a failure to achieve" an adequate return on the resources invested, because of renewed hostilities, implementation difficulties, shortfalls in donor financing, and the like; (b) risks to the Bank's reputation associated with the perception of failure in project implementation or of bias; and, (c) security risks to Bank staff working in post-conflict countries. To better manage these risks, the Bank must move into post-conflict countries in concert with other international actors such as bilateral donors, the European Union (EU), and UN agencies, restricting itself to its areas of comparative advantage, such as rehabilitation of infrastructure, advice on economic policy, aid coordination, institution building, and investments in the social sectors. Before intervention, the Bank must seek up-front, high-level agreements, both with key donors on the program and aid coordination arrangements and with relevant country authorities on their reciprocal responsibilities.

Guidelines for the Timing and Scale of Bank Involvement

The new framework provides a mechanism for the Bank to become involved in post-conflict countries in an informed manner. Trigger points for moving in and out of a particular phase ease some of the constraints on the Bank's capacity to respond expeditiously. The following guidelines have been developed to facilitate the timing and scale of the resumption of Bank programs following the conclusion of conflict.

A five-stage process is outlined, corresponding to various phases of post-conflict reconstruction:

- A watching brief in countries in conflict where there is no active portfolio
- Preparation of a transitional support strategy as soon as resolution is in sight
- Early reconstruction activities, proceeding as soon as field conditions allow
- Post-conflict reconstruction (under emergency procedures)
- A return to normal lending operations.

Stage I: A Watching Brief in Conflict Countries

A watching brief is needed during the conflict, when no active portfolio is possible, to keep track of developments and build a knowledge base that will be useful in preparing effective and timely Bank interventions once the conflict has moved toward resolution.

Where an active portfolio exists, the Bank's knowledge base develops in the course of normal operations. Analysis of the factors that affect development is mandated and budgeted through ongoing country assistance strategies and economic and sector work, as well as through day to day operations. A separate watching brief is not needed in these countries. A watching brief is needed only where normal working relations with the Bank are disrupted and incremental Bank budgetary and staff resources are needed.

A watching brief has four main objectives: to develop an understanding of context, dynamics, and needs so that the Bank is well positioned to support an appropriate investment portfolio when conditions permit; to evaluate the comparative advantages of institutions, including NGOs, operating in the relief phase, in order to identify implementing partners in reconstruction; to consult with humanitarian agencies on the long-term implications of short-term relief strategies; and to counter the adverse economic and environmental problems resulting from refugee and other spillover effects on neighboring countries in conflict.

During this period, judgments about the opportunities and risks associated with a higher level of activity would be made and updated continuously.

Stage II: A Transitional Support Strategy

When it becomes clear that there are opportunities for useful interventions, the responsible Bank regional office would propose to the Operations Committee the preparation of a transitional support strategy. This proposal would indicate the expanded requirements of the planning process (staff time and so on) and would provide relevant information regarding changes in a country's situation and its partnership with the United Nations and other actors. Approval of the proposal would trigger the activities outlined in stage II. The Executive Directors would be consulted at this stage through an information note; they may then request a discussion.

During this stage, Bank staff would initiate a process of detailed assessment and planning that would, assuming no deterioration of the situation, culminate in such a strategy. The Bank would participate in preparing a national recovery plan in collaboration with the government and other major partners in reconstruction. The direction of the program, the extent of the Bank's involvement, and risk-management strategies would be worked out by the country team. Assessment and planning during stage II should determine the direction and scale of the planned transition program. An allowance for this part of the Bank's work should be explicitly made in the administrative budget.

The transitional support strategy presented to the Operations Committee would include a clear statement of risks as well as strategies for entry and exit and recommendations of regional management on how the envisaged activities would be financed. Approval of a transitional support strategy would depend on the fulfillment of three basic preconditions: sufficient indication that a sustainable cease-fire has been or will be achieved shortly; presence of an effective counterpart for the Bank; and strong international cooperation with a well-defined role for the Bank. The support of other donors could be gauged by the resources mobilized. After the strategy is approved by the Operations Committee, it would be submitted to the Executive Directors for their endorsement.

The transitional support strategy submitted to the Executive Directors would include details as to how the overall proposal will be financed. Where possible, the proposed activities would be funded under normal Bank instruments. In some countries, undisbursed amounts may still be available under existing loans or credits, or there may be alternative sources, such as grants under the Institutional Development Fund (although these are limited in purpose and amount).[3] In other instances, Social Funds represent important instruments. If no sources are available quickly, either because of the time required to prepare a lending operation or, in some countries, because of nonmembership or nonaccrual status, the Bank may seek alternative funding mechanisms. In the cases

---

[3] The Institutional Development Fund (IDF) is a World Bank grant facility designed to finance capacity building for upstream and innovative institutional development activities that are not directly linked to ongoing or planned Bank operations but are in line with objectives outline in Country Assistance Strategies.

of Bosnia and Herzegovina and the West Bank and Gaza, for example, special trust funds were established, and allocations were made out of surplus. Where special funds are required to implement the transitional strategy, an accompanying recommendation would be made to the Executive Directors to this effect. Upon the endorsement of the strategy by the Executive Directors and their approval of any special funding, the early reconstruction phase would begin.

Stage III: Early Reconstruction Activities

Early reconstruction activities would be initiated as opportunities arise. They would be small-scale activities that can be undertaken relatively quickly—in many cases by or in partnership with UN agencies or NGOs—and would not be heavily dependent on normal Bank project preparation procedures. Small-scale activities during this phase, in addition to representing a response to urgent needs, can function as pilot activities that enhance learning for the design of later, larger-scale programs. Activities appropriate during this phase might include urgent repair of vital infrastructure; urgent demining; demobilization, including reintegration of ex-combatants; design of social safety nets in a post-conflict situation; small-scale and microenterprise credit schemes to restart production and promote employment; schemes to promote employment through infrastructure rehabilitation, small-scale construction, and reconstruction (social funds); start-up and recurrent costs of an emerging administration; technical assistance for restoring central and local government capacity; and planning and implementation of programs to create the conditions for reintegration of populations displaced by the conflict. Indicative planning for full-scale post-conflict reconstruction activities (stage IV) should begin during this period.

This initial operational involvement poses certain risks and represents the pivotal phase of Bank activity. To mitigate these risks, all parties to the conflict, as well as other international or nongovernmental agencies, may need to participate in the choices that the Bank makes. Before entering into activities in this phase, certain conditions must be met. The roles of various international agencies should be understood and agreed upon. Active conflict must have diminished to the point where Bank work can begin, and there should be a reasonable expectation of continuing relative stability or of a sustainable formal cease-fire. In addition, the Bank should have some presence on the ground and/or a satisfactory knowledge of the country, including an established dialogue with potential partners. The impact of the conflict on the economy, on communities, and on institutions should make immediate assistance necessary in order to develop an overall reconstruction program. The Executive Directors must agree, in the case of nonmembers, that assistance is warranted "for the benefit of members" and that there is an intention on the part of a nonmember country to become a member. Finally, the Bank must be satisfied that there is a commitment by the civil authorities to work with the Bank on reconstruction and development issues and that there is in place an administration capable of handling the in-country implementation aspects of Bank-funded work, with selective support by organizations such as the UN system, the EU, bilateral agencies, or NGOs.

The Bank, in partnership with other donors, should be prepared to move incrementally during this phase—that is, where certain areas have become peaceful, and provided that other conditions are acceptable, the Bank should assist with reconstruction in those areas.

Stage IV: Post-Conflict Reconstruction

As soon as large-scale operations are possible (that is, when there has been sufficient time to prepare for project preparation and/or to resolve any membership or arrears questions), they may be carried out under either normal or emergency procedures. Where security conditions and government commitment allow, support would include physical reconstruction, economic recovery, institution building, and social reintegration. An incremental, flexible approach, moving ahead as and when possible, would also allow activities to start before all donor funding can be made available. Funding would shift from special to regular sources—that is, to loans or credits from the International Bank for Reconstruction and Development (IBRD) and IDA.

Stage V: Return to Normal Operations

Throughout the process, but particularly when the emergency phase is over, and operations are once more carried out under normal lending procedures, and the consciousness of conflict begins to wane, the country assistance strategy and economic and sector work should explicitly recognize the effects of the conflict and the sometimes permanent transformation of society that may make the return to the status quo ex ante impossible and even undesirable. These documents should spell out what is needed to ensure that future operations not only do not exacerbate existing tensions but also contribute in a positive way to growth with equity. They need to include social assessments that can address some of the fundamental issues related to the aftermath of conflict . As noted, this recommendation also applies to country assistance strategies generally, particularly in countries viewed as "at risk."

Recommendations for Bank Operations

Field Presence and Partnerships

Field presence is essential to monitor, to maintain coordination with other donors, and to respond flexibly to changes. Bank resident missions need to be strengthened to meet post-conflict roles. The devolution of authority to managers in the field has proved to be a critical aspect of Bank programs in the West Bank and Gaza and in Bosnia and Herzegovina and should be considered strongly for other countries where local dynamics are similarly complicated and in flux.

The Bank's responsibility and its core relations are with member states. With due consideration for this fact, partnerships with UN and other donor agencies need to be forged as soon as possible in post-conflict phases. International NGOs often play a critical role in delivering services in post-conflict situations. The Bank can play an important role in strongly supporting the transition from implementation by international NGOs to indigenous responsibility as a post-conflict government resumes its welfare responsibilities.

Relief-Reconstruction Linkages

As a development agency, the Bank's main contribution in this area is likely to be in helping to close the gap between relief and development. Fostering a better understanding of the operational implications of this transition would help avoid negative patterns that can jeopardize later reconstruction and development activities. The Bank itself should have a clear appreciation early in the process of how its activities will engage and take over from emergency operations. The Bank should initiate contacts with relief agencies and with other international agencies, such as the UN High Commissioner for Refugees (UNHCR) and the International Committee of the Red Cross (ICRC), in the early phases of humanitarian assistance.

Aid Coordination

Effective coordination in a reconstruction program requires both cooperation and leadership. The Bank has provided leadership to donors that are providing development assistance in many post-conflict operations. In other situations the United Nations Development Programme (UNDP) or some other agency has played the key role of coordinator. Early agreement should be reached at a high level on the respective roles of the main players and especially on which will have the lead role in each sector. There are strong indications that the overall response of the international community would be enhanced by cohesive multidonor funding strategies.

New Operational Guidelines

Existing guidelines will be implemented flexibly and reviewed and revised as needed to ensure that Bank procedures facilitate an appropriate and efficient response in light of the experience gained from Bank operations in key post-conflict countries. For example, emergency lending procedures may need to be modified for the special circumstances of post-conflict countries—in particular, diminished government capacity and the uncertain dynamics of reconciliation and unification.[4] Revised procedures that may be indicated include streamlined procurement, audit, and disbursement that incorporate lessons from recent post-conflict reconstruction experience. The study of past Bank experience in certain conflict countries now being undertaken by the Operations Evaluation Department (OED) will provide guidance for areas where specific revisions might be required. Following the completion of that study in the summer of 1998, the issue of developing new operational guidelines for post-conflict situations will be revisited, and recommendations for further action will be made.

Implications for Bank Resources

The Bank will continue to rely primarily on its existing staff and structures at the country and regional levels:

---

[4] The Bank's policy on emergency recovery assistance, set out in Operational Policy 8.50 (OP/BP 8.50), details procedures for quickly disbursing emergency assistance for member countries. A country may request assistance from the Bank when it is struck by an emergency that seriously dislocates its economy and calls for a quick response from the government and the Bank. The main objectives of emergency recovery assistance are to restore assets and production levels in the disrupted economy. The policy notes, in this context, that the Bank finances investment and productive activities, rather than relief or consumption, and focuses on areas of its comparative advantage.

- *Country teams* in conflict countries are the first line in post-conflict activities and would need to have assured resources for the watching brief, for planning and assessment, and for the early phases of reconstruction.
- Small *regional teams* may be indicated. The impact of conflict is felt across national borders, and solutions often require the involvement of neighboring states. Moreover, conflicts may have region-specific aspects (economic transition in Europe and Central Asia, endemic poverty in Africa, and so on) that should be taken into account in the Bank's response. The decision to form a regional post-conflict team should rest squarely with the regional management team.
- A *Post-Conflict Unit* has been established within the Bank. It is to act as a focal point for handling contacts with other institutions, advising and briefing senior management, collecting information and monitoring country developments, and, drawing on experience from throughout the Bank, to accelerate the institutional learning process and disseminate information. These functions cannot continue to be carried out under the current ad hoc arrangements. To maximize the use of existing resources, some staff already working in post-conflict reconstruction will be consolidated in a small unit with limited terms of reference. The Post-Conflict Unit is located in the Social Development Department of the World Bank.

The resource requirements of post-conflict countries can far exceed those of other developing countries of similar size, and the impact on the Bank's administrative budget is considerable. In addition to any special initiatives associated with the implementation of this framework, it must be recognized that the costs of doing business in conflict countries are likely to be higher than in other countries. The new framework does not affect the largest part of the administrative cost of postwar reconstruction, but it would remove some uncertainty and facilitate upstream information about the needs of countries likely to emerge from conflict. The incremental costs of the new framework would be incurred in maintaining a watching brief in the five or six countries still in conflict where there is no Bank presence, carrying out assessment and planning when feasible, and supporting the incremental costs of the Post-Conflict Unit.

1
Post-Conflict Reconstruction in Context

The World Bank has always had a role in addressing the consequences of violent conflict; its original mandate was to support the reconstruction of Europe after World War II. The nature, scale, and proliferation of conflicts in the post–cold war era, however, are challenging development goals in a wide range of countries, threatening national and regional stability, and increasingly diverting international attention and resources from global development problems. In response, the international community is employing a range of relief, peacemaking, and peacekeeping initiatives, alongside reconstruction and development measures, and is exploring new mechanisms for coordination. The Agenda for Peace developed by the Secretary General of the United Nations and the request made by major donor countries at the Halifax summit to the Bretton Woods institutions (the World Bank and the International Monetary Fund) and the United Nations "to establish a new coordination procedure . . . to facilitate a smooth transition from the emergency to the rehabilitation phase of a crisis, and to cooperate more effectively with donor countries" represent prominent examples of this renewed interest in post-conflict reconstruction.

The Bank's commitment to assist countries emerging from conflict has been confirmed in several public statements, including the President's speech at the 1995 Annual Meetings. Although the costs and risks of increasing Bank activity are high, the costs and risks of inaction on the part of the international community can be prohibitive. Lack of understanding of conflict-related situations and lack of experience are substantial constraints, but the Bank has often proved nimble and innovative when called on to help. Risks can be addressed through judicious decisions about timing, type of intervention, and exit strategies. The financial costs of reconstruction can be large, requiring the concerted effort of the international community, including the Bank. This said, the Bank needs to consolidate its learning and more clearly define its evolving role to ensure that its comparative advantage is put to its best use within the international community and that its operations realize the potentially high returns to reconstruction activities.

In this evolving context, this report first reviews the extent of the problem in terms of its impact on international development efforts. Then, recognizing that conflicts rarely follow a smooth progression from escalation to resolution, the factors that can precede, sustain, or reignite conflict are briefly discussed. Subsequent sections deal with the need for integration of the issue of conflict prevention into the overall development paradigm, the challenges of post-conflict reconstruction, and the roles of various players that are part of the international response. The report summarizes Bank experience to date and reviews its emerging role in post-conflict reconstruction and its strengths and weaknesses in fulfilling this role. Finally, it makes recommendations to improve Bank responsiveness to the realities of post-conflict situations.

For Bank staff working with post-conflict countries and countries emerging from conflict, the report aims to provide a conceptual and operational framework within which to develop an appropriate response (box 1). At the same time, it encourages ingenuity, creativity, and initiative appropriate to individual country situations. Although there is a strong focus on post-conflict countries, where special efforts are required, the overall discussion of conflict and its relationship to development has broad implications for a wide range of countries. The purpose is not to prescribe a standard or comprehensive response but to outline the factors that should be considered in dealing with operational issues and in creating a capacity to respond. The report builds on the considerable work already completed by the Bank (see the References at the end of

---

Box 1 What Is Post-Conflict Reconstruction?

Post-conflict reconstruction supports the transition from conflict to peace in an affected country through the rebuilding of the socioeconomic framework of the society. Given the nature of intrastate conflict, the formal cessation of hostilities does not necessarily signify the completion of a process of transition, although it does represent a critical point in the transitional path. Reconstruction supports forward motion along this path.

Reconstruction does not refer only to the reconstruction of physical infrastructure. Nor does it necessarily signify a rebuilding of the socioeconomic framework that existed in a country prior to the onset of conflict. Conflict, particularly long-lasting conflict, transforms societies, and a return to the past may not be possible or desirable. Often, the inequities and fragility of the economies and weak governance structures of such societies have played a significant role in creating the conditions for conflict. In such cases what is needed is a reconstruction of the *enabling conditions* for a functioning peacetime society in the economy and society and in the framework of governance and rule of law. Conflict management and, where possible, reconciliation are threads that must run through this framework to achieve a sustainable result. The role of external agencies, including the Bank, is not to implement this process but, rather, to support it.

the book), and on discussions in the context of the Bankwide Working Group on Post-Conflict Reconstruction. In many ways, the objective is as much to raise questions as to provide answers. These proposals are not meant to provide a uniform response to conflict but to develop an institutional capability to treat each conflict situation according to its own characteristics. The issues will be reviewed and, if necessary, policies revised as the experience of the Bank and its partners widens.

The Impact of Conflict

The world has seen more conflicts in the past 20 years than in any other time in this century. Over 50 countries have been involved in major protracted intrastate conflict since 1980. In some 30 low- and middle-income countries, conflicts are in progress or have only recently ceased. Several other countries are under severe threat. About 35 million people are currently displaced as a result of conflict. In 30 countries, more than 10 percent of their population has been dislocated, and in 10 countries the proportion is more than 40 percent. The sheer numbers are only part of the story; in many cases this displacement has persisted over an entire generation or longer and will have serious long-term effects. Conflict has become a major constraint on alleviation of poverty; it has halted progress and has driven countries backward. For example, real per capita income in Lebanon in 1990 was estimated at about one-third its 1975 level; in Bosnia and Herzegovina, postwar incomes were about one-fourth of 1990 incomes, in dollar terms. The effects of conflict are particularly severe in Africa, where virtually every country has either experienced significant conflict or borders on another country in conflict. The proportion of official development assistance devoted to relief increased from 2 percent in 1989 to around 10 percent in 1994. Across the globe, peacekeeping operations alone cost the international community $3 billion in 1995. These increased relief and peacekeeping needs have inevitably affected development assistance. Reconstruction of countries emerging from conflict represents one of the major challenges for development agencies in the coming decades.

The legacies of conflicts include widespread population displacement; damaged infrastructure, including schools, health facilities, housing, and other buildings; reduced productive capacity; a devastated government revenue base; an erosion of human and social capital; greatly reduced security; and an increased proportion of people needing social assistance. Increasingly, land mines prevent access to infrastructure, agricultural land, and other productive facilities. Collectively, these legacies place a heavy burden on post-conflict societies. Conflict affects societies in a variety of profound and far-reaching ways that weaken their ability to complete the transition from war to a sustainable peace. Many countries emerging from conflict were poor in infrastructure and wealth even before going into conflict, but violence and civil strife break down the underpinnings of the economy, undermine predictability and confidence in the future, and disrupt markets, distribution networks, and banking and credit systems. Civil life is replaced by widespread militarization. Displacement denies access to previous livelihoods and to basic services. Gender roles are altered. Social organization and family units break down or become adapted to the new environment. Lack of trust in most institutions is prevalent. Wholesale adaptation to militarization or displacement becomes an obstacle to a smooth return to normal productive activities. If conflicts go on for a long time—and 20 countries have experienced warfare lasting 10 years or more—entire generations may mature under conflict conditions.

Conflict can destroy, in a short time, human capital gains and development investment that took decades to accumulate. Hard data on the extent of destruction are scarce and unreliable, but damage estimates from civil war in Lebanon have been as high as $25 billion; the total cost of three months of violent conflict in Rwanda, including relief costs, has been estimated at the equivalent of over a decade of official development assistance; and in Bosnia and Herzegovina the costs of peacekeeping and relief alone amounted to at least $10 billion. Economic ties with neighboring countries are disrupted, and market niches are lost. In addition to the severe direct human toll, there are other high costs of state failure and conflict that affect all aspects of development. For example, in Angola, sleeping sickness is again becoming a major problem because lack of access has hampered disease control programs.

There is no easy answer as to why conflicts occur or why they occur at a particular point in a country's history. Nor is it clear why some societies have weathered periods of tension and nascent conflict while others have broken down. What is clear is that conflicts are both a cause and an effect of impoverishment; 15 of the world's 20 poorest countries have experienced significant periods of conflict since the 1980s. But wealthier countries experience conflict as well. Conflict situations that might otherwise subside are frequently turned into conflagrations by the actions of external actors or local political entrepreneurs. Many (but not all) recent conflicts have a manifestation in ethnic or religious competition, but the underlying factors are more complex and involve economic, social, and political relationships. Often, conflicts are linked to competition for scarce resources, and in this context development strategies can play a role in enhancing or reducing tensions under particular circumstances. No conflict explodes due to one of these variables alone, but invariably occurs through a sequence of events.

Of particular significance, however, is the fact that most current conflicts occur not through the process of external war but rather through intrastate conflict. In most instances conflicts have arisen as a result of a breakdown of a society's institutional processes for peaceful dialogue and resolution of problems. In other cases, the withdrawal of the external support system after the end of cold war rivalries led to resurfacing of these conflicts and, in some cases, to "failed" states. Failed states are not all poor, as Lebanon, Yugoslavia, and parts of the former U.S.S.R. demonstrate. Conflict may be a consequence of economic change—of growth, as well as contraction. Trends such as powerful global information linkages, the spread of democratization across countries, and freedom of expression within national boundaries can serve either to dampen or to stimulate conflict, depending on individual circumstances.

Many developing countries with a fragile resource base, growing populations, and weak mediating institutions are likely to be confronted with competing demands by different population groups for control of shrinking national resources. In the absence of in-built mechanisms to resolve these demands amicably, there is a risk that conflict will result. The management of these conflicts is becoming an international collective responsibility. Along with the increase in intrastate conflict has come the concomitant phenomenon of countries attempting to traverse the path of a transition out of conflict. The Bank, as a key actor in the international community, must position itself, within its development mandate, to be able to respond to the challenge of investing in societies emerging from conflict and facilitating successful transitions to sustainable peace.

Development Assistance and Conflict Prevention

The World Bank and other development institutions need to better understand the nature of violent conflict associated with the paralysis or even dissolution of the state and the accompanying social and economic disintegration. It may be unrealistic to expect development agencies to prevent conflicts from occurring. The dynamics of conflict are not clearly understood. There is no single pattern or single causal agent in any given case, and outside actors have only a limited ability to influence the course of events in specific countries. Nonetheless, conflict represents lost opportunities as countries move away from the path of development. Societies that break down cannot grow, invest, and move forward. As the current situation in Burundi demonstrates, conflict often debilitates a society even without a complete collapse of the state. All types of civil violence (for example, urban crime and homicides in Colombia), have far-reaching effects on all facets of socioeconomic life.

Much of this report deals with the operational requirements of supporting the transition from situations of conflict to a sustainable peace. But some consideration must also be given to the importance of the causes and prevention of conflicts, for two reasons. First, conflict is cyclical. Many countries have returned to conflict after unsuccessful attempts at reconstruction; and reconstruction itself must take into account the dynamics of conflict and the inequities and schisms that led to breakdown in the first place. Long periods of hostility also create dynamics of their own (militarization, displacement, fragmentation of the state) that provide fuel for additional conflict. Second, prevention of conflict, where possible, is a far less costly alternative. Reconstruction is a very expensive process, which can never hope to rebuild all that is lost during conflict. The process of transition is long and painful and leaves scars that take generations to heal. Reacting to fires after they are set seems to be an unsatisfactory response.

But what can external actors do to address conflict, not only in the aftermath of violence, but before large-scale violence takes place? There is no easy answer, and prevention is not always possible. Yet, the lack of ready answers should not prevent concerted efforts to understand and prepare for potential opportunities to support societies in their efforts to avoid conflict. In any given situation, there are opportunities for external actors to have important effects on the shape of events. But these windows are difficult to predict ahead of time and must be dealt with on a case-by-case basis. Some donors have developed lists of countries at risk, and there is often talk of "early warning systems." It is, of course, important to identify situations in which the risk of conflict is heightened, but foreknowledge of tensions, in and of itself, does not guarantee a successful strategy to halt conflict. Nonetheless, recognition of the early manifestations of rising conflict may, in specific circumstances, provide windows for investments that could prove pivotal.

The true challenge is to integrate a sensitivity to conflict into the vision of development. Box 2, which reflects the discussion within the World Bank Task Group Report on Social Development and Results on the Ground, suggests some instruments that are useful not just for a few countries designated as already in conflict but for all countries in which the Bank does business. To a great extent, these are areas that the World Bank is already integrating into its operations but that can be consolidated and enhanced by further reflection and focus. These areas of analysis do not replace a focus on economic growth and comparative advantage. Rather, they enhance the potential for sustainable growth, permit the full utilization of a society's comparative advantages, and help to ensure that development interventions do not inadvertently fuel existing conflict and at the same time take advantage of existing opportunities to support stability within a given society.

Box 2 Some Ways of Integrating Concern for the Prevention of Conflict into Development Operations

Social assessments, including explicit recognition of sources of social conflict and social tension, as a core aspect of development planning. The analysis should focus on patterns of distribution of resources within a society and emphasize inclusiveness of opportunities, including attention to disparities among geographic regions or readily identifiable social groups.

Engagement with civil society, incorporating an approach to development that values participatory approaches and the concept of social capital, that is, the vision is that social organizations matter—that individuals make decisions reflecting their membership not only in households but also in larger social entities. The intermediary role of social organizations can support a stable environment for development or can prove to be the channel for organized violence that disrupts societies. Social capital, like any other form of capital, can be wisely or foolishly invested, used for many different ends, or squandered and wasted. In other words, evaluations of development investments must take full account of the fact that institutions and social organizations matter both for good and bad and provide the filters through which investments are distributed.

Increased focus on governance, incorporating provisions for accountability and transparency and including a heightened sensitivity to the role of government institutions in selectively allocating and extracting resources and in providing the predominant legal framework for dispute resolution and conflict management within the territorial boundaries of a given state.

A frank exploration of the costs of both random and organized violence in undermining the routine functions of socioeconomic activity. The impact of violence and the dissolution of bonds of trust and confidence in a society conflict with the underpinning assumptions of development and alter strategies of household accumulation and investment, yet are little understood.

The International Response

The international response to conflict situations incorporates four broad fields of activity that span post-conflict phases. These areas of activity, outlined in Annex B, together with the roles of some of the major international actors are:

- *Political-diplomatic.* Conflict resolution (for example, peace negotiations) and reconciliation; conflict avoidance, in particular demilitarization. The major actors are key governments acting bilaterally or multilaterally through influential alliances and multinational forums such as the United Nations, the North Atlantic Treaty Organization (NATO), the EU, and the Organization for Security and Cooperation in Europe (OSCE).

- *Security.* Peace operations, including peacekeeping to prevent violent confrontation and provide security for relief and rehabilitation. (Peacekeeping forces are usually supplied by individual governments through the United Nations, NATO, or some other arrangement.)
- *Relief or emergency aid.* Provision of basic necessities and, to the extent possible, maintenance of human and social capital. Donor states supply these mainly through agents such as the UNHCR, the United Nations Children's Fund (UNICEF), European Community Humanitarian Office (ECHO), and the World Food Programme (WFP), but bilaterally as well. NGOs are also significant contributors.
- *Aid for reconstruction and development.* Rebuilding economic and physical infrastructure, strengthening institutional capacity, and providing a base for sustainable development. The main providers are the EU, UN agencies such as the UNDP, donor states, NGOs, and international financial institutions (IFIs), including the regional development banks, the World Bank, and the IMF.

International experience in these four broad areas is still evolving, and the links between them are not well defined. Although the areas are conceptually different, activities may take place simultaneously. The areas are more "spheres of activity" than stages, and their implementation is interlinked. For example, the security provided by international peacekeeping forces may provide the stability and confidence necessary for beginning demilitarization and reconstruction, and the provision of food to populations affected by war should be linked to the timing of their reintegration and to development programs intended to rehabilitate agricultural land and housing. Aid programs without adequate security have often failed. Institutional mandates may not cover all aspects of the necessary responses. For example, most agencies maintain a distinction between relief and reconstruction activities, tending to leave a functional and budgetary gap that is not always closed by coordination mechanisms, and the international response may be hampered by unclear or overlapping mandates.

There are serious shortcomings in the present arrangements for aid coordination in reconstruction, as evidenced by fragmentation of assistance and large administrative burdens. The overlaps and gaps in mandates and the sheer number of actors (Rwanda attracted 7 major UN agencies, at least 200 NGOs, and all the major donors) can exacerbate confusion and induce delays. The burden imposed on a recipient country's new and inexperienced administration by separate demands from a multiplicity of donors weakens its capacity to implement. A key problem is that the international community is often ill equipped to respond quickly on the ground. Pledges are made rapidly, but commitment takes longer, and there is a considerable lag before actual disbursement takes place. Sustainable transitions out of conflict take several years, yet there is a tendency for donors to disengage once the conflict has receded from public attention.

Some of the problems with and consequences of donor aid coordination identified from recent experience are:

- Donor preference for bilateral programs leads to fragmentation of assistance and a large administrative burden on the recipient.
- Preference for tied aid gives rise to supply-driven programs.
- Preference for certain sectors, types of expenditure, or geographic areas means that some major sectors may remain unfunded; recurrent costs are rarely financed.
- Bureaucratic approval and procurement procedures lead to delays in commitment and disbursements.
- Weak in-country donor representation and coordination on the ground contribute to delays.

Donors, aid agencies, and policy institutions are working on various aspects of the response to conflict. For example, a task force of the Development Assistance Committee (DAC) of the Organisation for Economic Co-operation and Development (OECD) has prepared guidelines for "Development Co-operation in Conflict: Prevention and Post-Conflict Recovery." These guidelines were influenced significantly by the conclusions of a DAC-sponsored multi-donor evaluation of emergency assistance to Rwanda completed in 1996 (box 3).

Of particular interest in the international community is increased recognition of the linkage between relief and development. Set up in 1992 as the Department of Humanitarian Affairs (DHA) to coordinate relief, the UN Office of the Coordinator for Humanitarian Affairs (OCHA) has had to extend its attention to early reconstruction activities.[1] The United Nations system as a whole, through its Consultative Committee on Programme and Operational Questions (CCPOQ) is considering the adoption of a strategic framework for operations in post-conflict systems. The EU is reconsidering the cost-effectiveness of separate institutional and financial arrangements for relief, rehabilitation, and develop-

---

[1] Several agencies traditionally involved in development have created emergency or transitional units to deal with the initial reconstruction phase. The UNDP, for example, has expanded its Division of Emergency Response and had provided it with a $50 million fund in support of catalytic investments in reconstruction. UNICEF has strengthened its Emergency Unit and has prepared a major report on the impact of armed conflict on children. The U.S. Agency for International Development (USAID) has created an Office of Transitional Initiatives (OTI), with a $30 million budget.

Box 3 The Transition from War to Peace: Lessons from Rwanda

A year-long multidonor evaluation of the international response to the Rwanda conflict revealed a number of lessons relevant to Bank activities (Steering Committee of the Joint Evaluation of Emergency Assistance to Rwanda 1996). Two stand out: lack of in-depth knowledge of the historical, political, social, and economic context of the crisis in Rwanda undermined the effectiveness of international intervention; and conditionality on economic restructuring exacerbated social tensions and undermined efforts to improve human rights through political conditionality.

These are among the findings from the evaluation:

- The failure of the international community as a whole to provide adequate support for the government has undermined future stability and development efforts.
- An essential element of reconstruction in the Rwandan situation must be the establishment of an effective system of justice through which the perpetrators of genocide are seen to be accountable.

Recommended measures include these:

- Develop rapid, flexible procedures for disbursing reconstruction funds along the same lines as procedures for emergency assistance.
- Delegate more authority and resources to field-level operations to design and fund projects that will have a quick effect.
- Channel a greater proportion of resources to local and central government agencies.
- Assist NGOs in developing and adopting a comprehensive code for addressing a wide range of policy and operational issues, including coordination and division of labor among NGOs, qualifications for relief workers, local capacity building, and appropriate exit strategies.
- Support assistance targeted to the most vulnerable groups, especially female-headed households, working through indigenous NGOs, as well as through governments.

---

ment. The IMF has endorsed the expansion of its policy on emergency assistance to include certain post-conflict situations. Conditionality attached to this assistance would be tailored to individual country circumstances and would include a statement on economic policies, a quantified macroeconomic framework (to the extent possible), and a statement of the authorities to move as soon as possible to an upper credit tranche stand-by extended arrangement or an ESAF agreement.

The World Bank focuses primarily on post-conflict reconstruction and subsequent development. Operations in countries emerging from conflict are a significant proportion of its portfolio. In 1985 the Bank was not active in Cambodia, Lebanon, Uganda, Angola, or Mozambique, but by 1995 it had significant programs either under implementation or in planning stages in all of these countries, as well as in the West Bank and Gaza and in new states such as Armenia, Azerbaijan, Bosnia and Herzegovina, Croatia, Eritrea, and Georgia. In 1994, 24 percent of IDA commitments (excluding those for China and India) went to countries that had undergone or were in the process of emerging from significant periods of intrastate conflict. The Bank's interest and involvement in post-conflict operations continues to grow. The traditional World Bank role in reconstruction is undergoing some elaboration in response to the increasingly complex problems of post-conflict countries, and increasing emphasis is being placed on understanding how external investment can avoid exacerbating conflict (box 4). The economic advisory

---

Box 4 Principles of World Bank Involvement in Post-Conflict Reconstruction

In formulating its framework for supporting transitions from conflict, the Bank is guided by the following principles, which are either self-evident or dictated by the Articles of Agreement:

- The Bank is an international organization with a mandate defined in its Articles of Agreement in terms of financing and facilitating reconstruction and development in its member countries. It is not a world government for borrowing countries, with an unlimited mandate.
- The Bank is not in charge of peacemaking or peacekeeping. These are functions of the United Nations and certain regional organizations. The Bank can, however, assist peace efforts indirectly, through its developmental mandate.
- Under the explicit provisions of its Articles of Agreement, the Bank does not question the political character of a member and does not interfere in the domestic political affairs of a member.
- The Bank does not operate in the territory of a member without the approval of that member. (Bank resources and facilities can, according to the Articles, be used only for the benefit of members.)
- The Bank is not a relief agency. IBRD's Articles define its purposes in terms of assisting the reconstruction and development of its members by financing or facilitating investment for productive purposes and promoting international trade, through loans and guarantees.*

---

* Grants are not provided for in the Articles but were added through interpretation, if made out of net income. However, under the Articles, all Bank decisions are to be guided by the purposes provided for in Article 1. The IDA Articles likewise define its mandate in terms of assisting the development of the less-developed territories among IDA's membership. IDA financing is to be made in the form of loans, but other forms of finance may be authorized under replenishment resolutions (as was the case under the resolution on the IDA-11 replenishment, which authorized also the making of grants). As in the case of the IBRD, all IDA decisions are to be guided by the purposes provided for in its Articles.

role of the Bretton Woods institutions is also being tailored to post-conflict situations. Here, the paramount purpose is to create a stable foundation for supporting conflict-affected countries through the transition period to a stage at which they can normalize domestic and international financial and economic relations and private economic actors can resume their activities.

Development Assistance in the Transition from War to Peace

It is difficult to overstate the challenges of post-conflict situations. Governments often incorporate uneasy coalitions of former adversaries, and it is unrealistic to expect the underlying conflicts that initially brought countries to war to be resolved quickly. Conflicts go through cycles and do not always manifest themselves in violence at all times. Nor do they end abruptly with the signing of peace accords. In most post-conflict countries, government capacity is seriously affected by the loss of skills and experience associated with violence and displacement. Government decisionmaking capacity is also confounded by the complexities of post-conflict politics—balancing power blocs, forging alliances, facing the uncertainty of elections, and so forth. In many cases the post-conflict government is struggling to set up, for the first time, the functions required of a new administration, or even a new state. Post-conflict countries also tend to have formidable debt problems: they are often highly indebted before the onset of crisis, unable to service their debt for the duration of conflict, and in a severely weakened economic situation after the conflict. Since access to external resources is important for most post-conflict countries' medium- and longer-term development, normalization of relationships with the IFIs and with Paris and London Club creditors is a crucial part of post-conflict reconstruction.

Post-conflict reconstruction has two main objectives: facilitating the transition from war to a sustainable peace and supporting economic and social development. In support of the first objective, the international community has become increasingly involved in providing a framework for peacemaking and peacekeeping. This framework needs to be supported by activities that help address the residues of prolonged conflict through promotion of nonviolent forms of dispute resolution and support of activities related to demobilization, demilitarization, and reintegration of war-affected people into civilian life. Projects should be designed to rebuild links (such as infrastructure) between former combatants, to give special attention to the areas most affected, and to ensure that all former combatants have a stake in the fruits of peace. The justification for these activities is as much to prevent a return to conflict or a breakdown in social order as it is to promote the development of the economy.

The second objective—supporting economic and social development—requires that a peacetime economy be rebuilt as soon as possible and that state-society relations be restored at all levels. Since international assistance will never be sufficient to completely rebuild a country after conflict, assistance must focus on recreating the conditions that will allow the private sector and institutions of civil society to resume commercial and productive activities. To this end, support may be needed for macroeconomic stabilization, for rebuilding viable financial institutions and appropriate legal frameworks, and for reconstruction of urgent transportation and communication infrastructure. These needs must be addressed simultaneously. There may be some opportunities for other economic reforms inherent in the reconstruction process, and these should be used to advantage to the extent feasible.

It is important to recognize that restoring the enabling conditions for a functioning peacetime society requires measures to address widespread displacement and other conflict-related social transformations. Traditional social safety nets may be unable to cope with the increased numbers in vulnerable groups. Changes in family structures have a major impact on economic recovery. Of particular concern are female-headed households—typically a large, vulnerable group in post-conflict situations—which often need targeted assistance, including reform of gender bias in property laws and access to credit. But women, in this context, must be viewed not merely as a potentially vulnerable group but rather as agents of change in transitions from wars in which most combatants are male. There are also strong indications that a focus on investment in women and women's associations, particularly in the context of supporting a transition from conflict, is an important strategy in its own right.

Frequent weaknesses in government implementing capacity, combined with a dearth of statistics and other organized sources of knowledge, may tend to favor decentralized development initiatives. Participatory approaches and community-based schemes, especially under the unique conditions of post-conflict reconstruction, are particularly valuable in helping to restore local capacity.

With these challenges in mind, and under the assumption that the necessary diplomatic/political and peacekeeping/security interventions are in place, the following priority activities need to take place during post-conflict reconstruction:

- Jump-starting the economy through investment in key productive sectors and supporting the conditions for resumption of trade, savings, and domestic and foreign investment, including macroeco-

nomic stabilization, rehabilitation of financial institutions, and restoration of appropriate legal and regulatory frameworks
- Reconstructing the framework of governance: strengthening government institutions, including capacity for resource mobilization and fiscal management; the restoration of law and order and the organizations of civil society.
- Repairing important physical infrastructure, including key transport, communications, and utility networks
- Rebuilding and maintaining key social infrastructure: that is, education and health, including the financing of recurrent costs
- Targeted assistance to the war-affected, that is, reintegration of displaced populations; demobilization and reintegration of ex-combatants; revitalization of the local communities most disrupted by conflict through support (such as credit lines) to subsistence agriculture, microenterprises, and the like; and support for vulnerable groups (such as female-headed households)
- Land mine action programs, including mine surveys, and demining of key infrastructure as part of comprehensive development strategies for supporting a return to normal life of populations living in mine-polluted areas
- Financial normalization: planning a workout of arrears, rescheduling of debt, and the longer-term path to financial normalization.

Because sustainable development depends heavily on peace building and visible "peace dividends," especially during the fragile early period, physical reconstruction and transitional initiatives may need to be undertaken before the larger economic reform program gets fully under way. Such initiatives can build trust and sustain confidence in a war-weary population during the often rocky transition to peace. They may also build confidence in private investors, both domestic and foreign, and thus help draw badly needed capital into the reconstruction process. Parallel with an appreciation of the need to act quickly within brief windows of opportunity, it is important to recognize that for any transition to be sustainable, post-conflict governments must begin to show their commitment to rational policies of reconstruction and sound macroeconomic policies early in the reconstruction process. Although it is difficult to assess this process, particularly during the early stages, care has to be taken so that early initiatives do not establish unsustainable precedents. Sustainability in this regard should include attention to the environmental consequences of long periods of conflict, which often result in short-sighted strategies for the use of natural resources. The sequencing of the various parts of the overall economic reform program with transition initiatives and the longer-term reconstruction program depends on specific country conditions, but careful thought should be given to their initial design. Special attention must often be paid to the variable effect of war on different regions of affected countries and to the implications for prioritization of investment.

2
Lessons from World Bank Experience

This report draws extensively on Bank experience across the globe. Many of the constraints on Bank operations have been highlighted by experience in many countries in Sub-Saharan Africa, including Angola, Burundi, Liberia, and Rwanda. Operations in two recent post-conflict situations, in the West Bank and Gaza and in Bosnia and Herzegovina, demonstrate the range of reconstruction issues that the Bank, at its very best, can address, creatively and effectively, within existing policy and operational procedures. Intensive international attention and political will have been key elements in facilitating the transition from conflict to peace in each case. These two situations, perhaps more than others, also demonstrate the enormous requirements, in staff time and financial resources, of post-conflict countries—a factor which, up to now, has not been uniformly allowed for.

In El Salvador and in Nicaragua, the Bank came relatively late to the process and there was insufficient political consensus on the objectives. In other post-conflict countries, particularly in Sub-Saharan Africa, where the international response has been weak or fragmented, it has often proved difficult for the Bank to operate at an appropriate level of involvement. By contrast, in Uganda, where a cohesive and popular government was able to manage the transition, the combined Bank-led assistance for macroeconomic policy formulation, civil service reform, demobilization, and programs targeted to vulnerable groups hastened recovery. The challenge for the Bank is to evaluate its response to post-conflict reconstruction worldwide in the context of increasing demands on shrinking resources and to assess the degree to which patterns developed in successful cases can be replicated elsewhere. A number of lessons have been learned, and they form the basis for recommendations concerning the Bank's current policies and procedures. These lessons focus on the role of the Bank as part of a multidonor response, the experience gained from operations, and the constraints faced in responding quickly.

Early Engagement

The need for early engagement in post-conflict situations is strongly indicated by Bank experience to date. Time is of the essence in post-conflict situations. Often, there are windows of opportunity within which significant progress is possible. But these windows can quickly narrow or close. In some instances, the Bank's absence from a conflict country for extended periods has restricted the institution's response capacity once the conflict has receded. The result has been loss of the opportunity to provide valuable support to transitional initiatives, as occurred in Liberia between 1989 and 1995. In at least 16 countries, Bank-supported efforts at post-conflict reconstruction began (or would in time begin) in a situation in which there has been little or no sustained, regular contact between the Bank and the affected country for five years or more.[1] Even absences during shorter but critical intervals (for example, Rwanda in 1994 and 1995) have had an impact on the Bank's ability to interact effectively with a new government. The lack of Bank presence in these situations adversely affected the ability of management and staff to recognize in a timely fashion opportunities to support the transition of a country out of conflict.

In general, when the potential for a successful transition from conflict has been recognized, the Bank has responded quickly and flexibly in initiating contact and preparing, or participating in the preparation of, a strategy and funding package. Often, this response has been made possible by the personal commitment and dedication of staff. In some cases (Angola, Armenia, Azerbaijan, Bosnia and Herzegovina, Cambodia, Croatia, Mozambique, and Rwanda, for example) residual hostilities did not prevent assessment and planning from being carried out; in others, such as the West Bank and Gaza, extensive preparatory work was done very early in the peace process. Managers and staff involved in these situations agree that in each case success was attributable to a complex interaction of extraordinary all-out efforts of country teams, the high profile of the cases, and a certain degree of good fortune. The outcome may not be fully replicable in other cases.

---

[1] The World Bank was absent for significant periods of time prior to reentry in Lebanon (15 years), Cambodia (20 years), and the West Bank and Gaza (23 years). In the past 10 years the Bank has begun new operations in seven countries in transition from conflict situations either due to their emergence as independent state (Azberbaijan, Bosnia and Herzegovina, Croatia, Eritrea, Georgia, and Namibia) or due to a change in situation allowing for the Bank-supported programs to be considered (Angola). The Bank has very recently begun preparation of support strategies for Liberia and the Democratic Republic of the Congo.

The lack of a government counterpart for the Bank when states collapse or fail and no clear authority emerges, as in Afghanistan or Somalia, clearly constrains the nature and size of the Bank's assistance program. In other cases, where the outcome is fairly clear, the Bank has creatively worked within the existing framework to provide resources to governments even before their states are recognized as formal members of the Bretton Woods institutions, as occurred with the emergency loan for Eritrea, via an agreement with the Ethiopian government. Other solutions were found in the cases of the Palestinian authority and Bosnia and Herzegovina.[2] In principle, IDA credits may be disbursed to agencies other than governments, facilitating early entry and offering the potential for development of pilot initiatives at the community or regional level if conditions otherwise seem favorable. There may be opportunities to work with subnational units, NGOs, or regional organizations even before the formation of a national government.

Doubts about the legitimacy of a government can hamper and delay effective donor response, coordination, and dialogue. The Bank's intervention in a post-conflict situation can take place at the request of the government in power. If more than one government asserts power, the Bank should follow its written policy on de facto governments. The crux of this policy is that the Bank does not make political choices but is guided by the actual situation (that is, who is in effective control) and the general recognition of the international community. If there is no government in power, Bank action (which, obviously, would not be in the form of loans) may be initiated by requests from the international community as properly represented—for example, by UN agencies—and subject in each case to the prior approval of the Board, where all Bank members are represented. The increasing problem of "stateless societies" or societies where there is no functioning state for long periods of time raises for the Bank and other development agencies important questions that require further reflection and study. The watching brief period proposed in the next chapter is an appropriate time for such work.

Presence in the Field

The need for a strong field presence is one of the clearest lessons to emerge from experience to date. Post-conflict situations are complicated and

---

[2] In the case of the West Bank and Gaza the Executive Directors agree the assistance to nonmembers was warranted "for the benefit of members." Bosnia and Herzogovina had declared its intention to become a member. Membership conditions were outlined in the Board's decision regarding eligibility for succession to the membership of the former Yugoslavia (Socialist Federal Republic of Yugoslavia). Funds for preparatory work were provided by the Netherlands.

involve a multitude of players and organizations. An expansion of field presence and field-level authority, such as has occurred in Bosnia and Herzegovina and in the West Bank and Gaza, allows a more flexible response and a deeper, country-specific understanding of the relevant dynamics of such situations. In the West Bank and Gaza some of the need for field presence has been met through halfway measures, such as the use of extended missions by task managers. Flexible arrangements of this kind offer potential benefits and may be of particular relevance where security conditions in a country make a permanent in-country residential presence inadvisable.[3] For some projects, particularly those involving a new activity, a new institution, or cooperation among several institutions, full-time presence in the field is needed for project appraisal and early supervision. A limited Bank field presence can be supported by partnerships with NGOs and UN agencies with significant presence in the country.

Adequacy of Existing Instruments

The economic and sectoral objectives to be supported by the Bank are normally outlined in the context of a Country Assistance Strategy. However, the uncertainties inherent in post-conflict situations, as underscored by recent experience in Bosnia and Herzegovina and elsewhere, suggest that a different approach is required, as it is not feasible to define an overall strategy a priori. A pragmatic and "opportunistic" approach is needed; building on what is feasible. Although certain preconditions may be necessary before the Bank undertakes certain kinds of activities, fragile political situations and often devastated economies make the development of rigid performance criteria unfeasible and inappropriate. Nonetheless, as noted above, if sustainable transitions are to succeed, post-conflict governments must demonstrate a willingness to pursue appropriate policies of economic management, arrears clearance, and the like within the constraints of transitional periods. Once it becomes feasible to undertake economic and sector work, including Country Assistance Strategies, these need to contain explicit analysis of the conflict factors in order to avoid accentuating inequities directly or indirectly through Bank investments. This would be in line with the stronger focus within the Bank on the social dynamics of development, stakeholder analysis, and increased participation in the development process.

---

[3] Relevant policies relating to Bank staff and security conditions in post-conflict countries (salaries, travel, insurance, and so on) need to be reviewed.

To be effective in a fragile post-conflict situation, resources have to be made available as soon as conditions on the ground allow and when the requirements change from relief-only to reconstruction. Early support would help to put post-conflict countries on a reconstruction and development track and would facilitate the development of a framework for mobilization and effective use of donor resources. In some countries, resources can be made available from undisbursed existing loans or credits. Development of new lending operations, however, takes time. Arrears to IBRD or IDA constitute an additional complication. Since access to resources from the Bank and other international financial institutions is important for most post-conflict countries' medium- and longer-term development, planning financial normalization is crucial. The extent of the arrears problem in several of the affected countries, such as Liberia, is significant. It should be noted, however, that the presence of arrears does not preclude the mobilization of assistance from donor countries, or the (nonlending) assistance of the Bank, for initial post-conflict reconstruction and recovery assistance. In such cases the Bank's close partnership with other agencies can provide avenues for critical first steps that can later be followed up by larger Bank initiatives. Normalization may take much longer, and, even after normalization, debt servicing will represent a daunting obstacle to rebuilding shattered economies, many of which had extremely limited growth potential even before the conflict. Long-term normalization for countries such as Afghanistan, Liberia, Somalia, and Sudan may be a major challenge for the entire international community. Solutions will depend on a variety of factors, including the size of the arrears and the amount of support available from the international donor community to assist with financing.

Much of the Bank's work in post-conflict reconstruction over the past decade has been in rebuilding physical infrastructure such as roads and buildings—a traditional area of strength—carried out under guidelines for emergency lending, as set out in OP/BP 8.50. Although such an approach is valid for reconstruction following natural disasters, post-conflict reconstruction requires a broader approach that takes into account the multifaceted impacts of long, violent conflict. Recent responses have also included operations specifically designed to promote economic adjustment and recovery, such as targeted employment creation programs. The promotion of employment, following years of combat and militarization, is important not only to begin the process of economic development but also to provide jobs to ex-combatants, displaced persons, and other people affected by war and to underpin a return to the routine of normal peacetime life. It is increasingly clear that in today's post-conflict societies the whole range of social sector needs has to be assessed, and means of support ensured, if valuable human capital is to be maintained. This means, for example, keeping educational and medical systems operational. As a tool for providing faster Bank processing of loans or credits, without the conditionality present in normal lending, emergency lending has been very useful for post-conflict reconstruction, as evidenced by its extensive use in Bosnia and Herzegovina. Still, the Bank's emergency guidelines were developed for a project-based response to natural disasters, not for the aftermath of intrastate conflicts; they thus represent an imperfect framework for response in post-conflict situations. Worldwide, during the 10 years 1985–95, 14 emergency projects were approved to support reconstruction in countries emerging from conflict. From 1995 to 1997, 16 additional emergency projects were approved for Bosnia and Herzegovina alone. For the first time in the history of the Bank, most of a portfolio in a country is being implemented under emergency provisions.

Investments in promoting a rational and dynamic private sector are a key aspect of supporting a vibrant post-conflict economy. Long periods of conflict have often led to distortions and inefficiencies in the economies of countries in conflict; monopolies on resource extraction may be dominated by individuals or warring factions, with little or no benefit to the public. Harnessing of the domestic resources available and the reemergence of an energetic private sector (and, consequently, of a domestic tax base for public sector expenditure) will be critical for successful post-conflict reconstruction. The International Finance Corporation (IFC) is moving in this area and has developed plans for some post-conflict countries. The role of the private sector in reconstruction needs careful consideration, because the private sector could provide critical underpinning for a transitional process in terms both of economic development and of job creation in war-damaged economies. The IFC, along with the Bank, has agreed to support the development of microcredit operations in the West Bank and Gaza. Other examples of note include natural resource mining projects in Sierra Leone and Tajikistan, and additional projects are in the pipeline. In Bosnia and Herzegovina the IFC is actively engaged in exploring possibilities for a venture capital project.

The Bank has also become involved in the following new areas of activity and has developed new lending operations in response to the particular challenges posed by post-conflict countries:

- *Demobilization and reintegration of ex-combatants.* The expertise developed in Africa, and described in a best practices paper (Colletta, Kostner, and Wiederhofer 1996b), is being drawn on elsewhere on an ad hoc basis (box 5). The Bank has played an important role in shaping multidonor investments in demobilization and reintegration in Uganda, Mozambique, Ethiopia, Cambodia and Sierra Leone. Demobilization programs have substantially decreased defense

---

**Box 5 Supporting the Transition from War to Peace:
The Uganda Veterans Assistance Program**

As part of its broader efforts to rehabilitate the economy and society following decades of warfare, the government of Uganda decided to shift the burden of its public expenditure away from defense and toward the social and economic sectors. It established the civilian Uganda Veterans Association Board (UVAB) to facilitate the demobilization and subsequent reintegration into productive civilian life of 36,400 soldiers of the National Resistance Army. The Uganda Veterans Assistance Program (UVAP) also took into account the needs of approximately 125,000 dependents who were resettled with the veterans. That program was implemented between 1992 and 1996 with assistance from donors, coordinated by the World Bank.

Veterans and their dependents constituted a particularly vulnerable group, and a potential threat to security, because of their lack of civic awareness, low skill levels and meager resources, and culture of dependency. UVAB assistance consisted of three components: demobilization, reinsertion assistance (a transitional safety net cash equivalent, to meet basic needs for a six-month period or one crop-growing season), and reintegration—in particular, counseling and training. Although it is too early to determine whether the long-term reintegration of veterans has been achieved, the recently completed program is widely hailed as a success. Political will, needs-based planning, and donor coordination through the World Bank culminated in timely and effective program completion.

Among the lessons learned from the program are the following:

- Preparatory studies, to determine the socioeconomic profile of the veterans (characteristics, needs, and aspirations) and assess the opportunities for veterans in product and factor markets and the institutional implementation requirements, are essential for appropriate program design.
- Issuance of a nontransferable discharge certificate ensures that veterans have access to their benefits and reduces the risk of targeting errors. The continuous provision of information to beneficiaries about opportunities, constraints, and procedures significantly enhances reintegration.
- It is the interplay of a community's physical and social capital and a veteran's financial and human capital that determines the ease and success of reintegration.
- Central coordination through a temporary agency, balanced by decentralization of implementation authority to the communities, makes for a powerful institutional arrangement. Field offices enable beneficiaries to have easier access to program benefits and allow the government to make the program more responsive to local needs.

---

expenditures in conflict countries, permitting funds to go toward pressing reconstruction needs. Reinsertion initiatives have strengthened peace processes, reduced tensions, and eased the transition to normalcy.

- *Reintegration of displaced populations.* Direct Bank involvement in this field has been relatively limited but is growing. Bank operations have been designed in partnership with and at the explicit request of the UNHCR and other relevant international agencies, in the hope of developing sustainable strategies that build on initial programs developed by relief agencies to facilitate the return home of refugees and internally displaced persons. The high degree of displacement and the increasing numbers of internally displaced persons in some countries makes directed resettlement programs impracticable or accessible only to specific concentrated groups of displaced people. Support for reintegration can also take the form of focused regional agricultural initiatives, development of legal frameworks for land distribution, dispute resolution, and the like. Large-scale displacement invariably has implications for the character of a wide range of economic and sector work and can be addressed only through integrated development programs.
- *Demining.* The recently approved internal guidelines for financing land mine clearance recognize the importance of dealing with land mine pollution as a prerequisite for many development activities. Mine pollution distorts the comparative advantage of various development initiatives, particularly in the transport and agriculture sectors; early mine survey is critically important in affected countries. Under the guidelines, support can be given to increase local capacity to deal with mines, through demining, training, surveying, and mine-awareness programs. The Bank's involvement in demining is an iterative process, and lessons are being learned as projects in various countries move through the stages of implementation. Mine-clearing projects or components of projects have been approved for Bosnia and Herzegovina and for Croatia, and projects with mine action components are under consideration for Angola, Azerbaijan, and Cambodia.

Coordination in the Transition to Peace

Peace treaties and their execution require coordination with reconstruction and economic stabilization measures to underpin their objectives. The Bank's expertise can be critical (as at the Dayton talks on Bosnia and Herzegovina), contributing a reconstruction and development perspective and providing practical advice on immediate matters such as the implications for economic governance, budgets, economic incentives, and so on of proposed government structures, taxation arrangements, and demilitarization and demobilization arrangements. Collaboration with the IMF on stabilization and other macroeconomic issues is an important part of this process. Early Bank involvement in the peace process (as recently occurred in Guatemala) also helps to ensure realistic planning on the part of the Bank and facilitates integration of the goals of the peace process into Bank strategies for economic management in a transitional period. Early consultations between the UN agencies responsible for peacekeeping and the Bretton Woods institutions are therefore indicated.

Given their respective mandates, there is a clear need for coordination very early on between the Bretton Woods Institutions and the providers of relief (see box 6 for an example). The importance of contact and consultation between relief and development agencies is strongly supported by the UNHCR, the ICRC, and other major international agencies involved in humanitarian operations. The Bank should not substitute for relief organizations or provide relief itself. This is not only a question of comparative advantage but also a requirement of the Bank's Articles. It is important, nonetheless, to recognize that relief and development agencies are often operating within their respective mandates during the same period in the same country. Relief can create dependency or introduce distortions that can have impacts on development-oriented policies; examples include food distribution that affects incentives for agricultural production, an extended emphasis on curative rather than preventative health care strategies, and high salaries paid to local staff by relief agencies that may create unrealistic expectations. There is increasing recognition in the international community that much better information sharing and coordination could prevent some of these adverse effects and facilitate a more efficient transition to sustainable development. The Bank should, therefore, where relevant, coordinate its work with that of relief agencies and inform them of potential Bank activities that may complement their work.

Operating within its mandate, the Bank can provide and has provided support to international efforts both in direct financing of post-conflict activities and in other nonlending roles. For example, the catalytic effect of Bank involvement in resource mobilization is well demonstrated by experiences in Bosnia and Herzegovina, Cambodia, Lebanon, Somalia, and the West Bank and Gaza. To date, perhaps the best example of an aid mechanism has been the Holst Fund for support of recurrent expenditures in the West Bank and Gaza program (box 7). The Holst Fund was used to channel funds to the emerging Palestinian administration in an efficient, transparent, and accountable manner.

In summary, although the Bank has often been quite flexible in adapting to the changing circumstances and new demands of the growing post-conflict portfolio, it is clear that there are areas where significant improvement is needed. As part of the international response, donor

---

Box 6 Afghan Refugees in Pakistan

Over a 12-year period beginning in 1984, the World Bank managed three Income Generating Projects for Refugee Areas (IGPRAs) with trust fund resources from bilateral donors on behalf of the UNHCR. Through nearly 300 subprojects in public works, forestry, and conservation, the IGPRAs provided much-needed employment, training and skills to Afghan refugees in Pakistan. The projects, which employed both Afghan refugees and local Pakistanis, helped mitigate some of the ecological damage to northern Pakistan caused by the presence of 3.5 million Afghan refugees and their livestock. A recent evaluation by the Bank's Operations Evaluation Department led to some important conclusions.

- The IGPRA program is a concrete example of how the Bank can, within its mandate, assist in development investments that have a positive impact on conflict-affected populations, without being directly involved in an area of continuing conflict. (Afghanistan has been in open conflict since 1979.)
- The IGPRAs illustrate a creative form of cooperation between the Bank, a UN agency, and a number of donor governments for assistance to displaced populations. They indicate one specific area in which the development experience of the Bank and its credibility can usefully complement the relief effort.
- The IGPRA program responded both to the needs of a refugee host country and to the long-term maintenance of human capital among refugees. This is one of the few documented cases in which assistance to refugees in the host country was not relief oriented. Instead, the focus was on income generation and development of skills that could also be useful for reconstruction programs after the refugees return to their native country and on a response to the regional impacts of conflict-induced displacement.

An important condition that made the IGPRA program successful in Pakistan was the cultural affinities between refugees and hosts. This fact has to be taken into consideration when applying such an approach to other countries with problems of displaced populations.

---

coordination needs a more unified project investment approach and procedures, faster disbursements, and longer-term commitment. With regard to Bank operations, country teams have, for the most part, responded creatively and effectively within the limits of existing institutional constraints. But given the rapidly increasing experience, the Bank's response should now begin to benefit from a more comprehensive view, as well as a guiding framework for operations. Some particular areas for improvement include earlier engagement to allow a more informed early response; the ability to carry out planning activities (using the Bank's own resources, without seeking donor support); greater field

Box 7 Reconstruction in the West Bank and Gaza

The Bank's program in the West Bank and Gaza began with a comprehensive strategic study of the Palestinian economy, at the request of the partners to the multilateral Middle East Peace initiative. The Bank then drew up a public expenditure program for the Palestinian territories. The West Bank and Gaza is not a sovereign entity and is therefore not eligible to borrow from the Bank. Bank operations were, however, made possible in October 1993 with the creation of a $50 million Trust Fund for Gaza, using Bank surplus (replenished in 1995 and in 1997 with a further $180 million in all and extended to cover the West Bank). Since then, the Board has approved 12 reconstruction credits on IDA terms and 1 grant. The Bank also administers two major multidonor trust fund projects. Worth noting are:

- *The Bank's central role in donor coordination.* This derived from a mandate to the Bank from Palestinians, Israelis, and donors to establish the parameters of the assistance program and from the Bank's formal role as chair of the Consultative Group, secretariat of the Ad Hoc Liaison Committee (a political-level committee of key donors, Israelis, and Palestinians charged with overseeing the donor program), and co-chair of a well-organized local aid coordination structure. Despite this role, and notwithstanding a high degree of political coordination, the implementation of the donor program has sometimes been cumbersome. With the main exception of the Holst Fund (see below), donors have tended to resist opportunities for cofinancing and close coordination across national or agency lines. This has led to a multitude of varying procedures that overtax the nascent Palestinian administration, although disbursement levels have been good overall.

- *The unprecedented success of the donors' recurrent budget support effort, the highlight of which has been the Bank-administered Holst Fund ($265 million pledged by 26 donors, of which $247 million is disbursed).* The Holst Fund is a pooled trust fund, managed by the Palestinian Authority under the close scrutiny of a field-based World Bank "agent"—an international accounting firm responsible for pre-audit inspection. Despite donors' traditional reluctance to provide budget support financing, the political leadership of the Ad Hoc Liaison Committee, combined with the trust fund experience of the Bank, proved attractive to donors. Pooling of the funds made for speed and for flexibility: in addition to playing a major role in sustaining the Palestinian administration in 1994–96, the Holst Fund financed a significant program of employment generation in 1996 and 1997, helping mitigate some of the harsher effects of border closure.

- *An evolving role for the Bank.* The first phase of Bank assistance also featured small-scale, visible infrastructure rehabilitation. To date, almost 1,000 Bank-financed schemes have been completed, creating well over 4 million person-days of work. With the Palestinian administration now beginning to gain experience, program emphasis is shifting to medium-term policy and institutional development work. A new generation of projects in support of private sector development, human resources, and systemic poverty alleviation have now been put in place.

- *The Bank's own structural reorganization, to increase effectiveness in the West Bank and Gaza.* The lack of Palestinian implementation capacity, combined with a fluid and unpredictable political environment, made for great difficulties in directing the Bank program from Washington. As a result, implementation lagged in 1993–94. In late 1995, principal program management responsibilities were devolved to a field-based country director, who is directly responsible to the regional vice president for the country strategy and program delivery. Tasks are managed either by a small, tightly-knit country department of four senior staff (two of whom are based in headquarters) or by the sector management units. As a function of this de-layering, and in response to the need for speed, task managers have been given considerable autonomy and have responded by cutting preparation time and costs on new operations.

presence; early information sharing with relief agencies to avoid negative development consequences and achieve better coordination with donors throughout the response; and a stronger focus on governance, participatory approaches, social assessment, and social policy.

3
A New Reconstruction Framework

The new reconstruction framework described in this chapter proposes a phased approach that permits the Bank to become involved in post-conflict countries in an informed manner. By employing trigger points for moving in and out of a particular phase, it eases some of the constraints that hinder the Bank's capacity to respond expeditiously. The elements of the proposed approach include a framework for the timing and scale of Bank involvement in post-conflict countries and a set of operational recommendations that include new procedural guidelines for post-conflict reconstruction activities. The framework largely consolidates recent Bank practice rather than breaking into new territory. It provides the logical structure for an increasing involvement appropriate to country circumstances but leaves strategy in the hands of country and regional teams. Crucial decisions regarding entry and exit would require approval of the Operations Committee and the Board. The framework requires Board consultation and guidance and presents options, as opposed to institutional imperatives, for Bank involvement.

The Five Stages of the Framework

The five-phase process set out below outlines a graduated series of steps through which the Bank can reestablish programs as a country moves out of conflict. The following types of involvement correspond to various phases of conflict and post-conflict reconstruction and will provide guidance for Bank operations in conflict countries (Annex A).

- A watching brief in conflict countries in which there is no active portfolio
- Preparation of a transitional support strategy as soon as resolution is in sight
- Transitional early reconstruction activities, proceeding as soon as field conditions allow
- Post-conflict reconstruction (under emergency procedures)
- Return to normal lending operations.

The Bank would move through these phases according to its assessment of risks. For example, if conditions deteriorate during the preparation of a transitional support strategy, the Bank would revert to a watching brief. The Executive Directors would be regularly informed and consulted about such changes as appropriate.

Before detailing the proposed phases of activity, it is necessary to reiterate the importance of Bank concern for the issue of prevention in "at-risk" countries. Although there can be no certainty about causes of conflict or the effectiveness of prevention, some underlying and triggering factors may allow identification of potential conflict countries. Rwanda and Burundi, for example, were designated as at-risk by some elements of the international community, including NGOs, before the onset of widespread violence. There is no clearly defined "stage" in which countries are at risk of undergoing debilitating conflict; rather, there are varying degrees of intrastate conflict. The appropriate concern for the World Bank is that, in any given situation, the goals of the programs (and the modalities for implementation of those goals) which it supports to promote sustainable development are achievable. The Bank's relationship is with the government of a member state, and, as noted in chapter 1, it will not interfere in the domestic political affairs of a member. Nevertheless, it should take steps to ensure that its project interventions and conditions do no harm—for example, that they do not aggravate existing inequities. Moreover, when requested to do so by a member, the Bank should consider supporting government attempts to promote activities aimed at ameliorating conditions that may lead to conflict. Such activities might involve attention to distributive policies; to policies and regulations that affect access to resources (credit, land) and opportunities (education, employment); and to participation of excluded groups. The series of points raised in box 2—explicit recognition of conflict as an issue in development, a focus on social capital and on the positive and negative intermediary role of social institutions, and increased emphasis on the framework of governance—are all aspects that, on a case-by-case basis, can enhance the relevance of the Bank's operations in countries with high risk of conflict. Moreover, the Bank's influence in the international community can help to support the integration of these aspects into external investment by other donors, as well as by sources in the private sector.

When a conflict has already begun and there is no active World Bank portfolio in a given country, the five stages provide a framework for Bank involvement. The pace and progression of a given country program through these stages will depend on local conditions, commitment by other donors, and other factors and will vary greatly from one situation to another.

Stage I: A Watching Brief in Conflict Countries

The purpose of a watching brief is to keep track of developments in countries in which no active portfolio is possible and to provide knowledge that will be useful in preparing effective and timely Bank-assisted operations once post-conflict reconstruction activities are possible. Where there is no active portfolio, the Bank should monitor conflict countries in order to:

- Develop an understanding of the context, dynamics, and needs so that the Bank is well positioned to support an appropriate investment portfolio when conditions permit
- Evaluate the comparative advantages of institutions, including NGOs, operating in the relief phase, to identify implementing partners in reconstruction
- Consult, particularly at the request of the United Nations, with humanitarian agencies on the long-term implications of short-term relief strategies
- Counter the adverse economic and environmental problems resulting from refugee and other spillover effects on states bordering on conflict countries.

Where an active portfolio exists, the Bank's knowledge base develops in the course of normal operations. Analysis of the factors that affect development is mandated and budgeted through ongoing country assistance strategies and economic and sector work, as well as through the day-to-day operations of programmatic activity. A separate watching brief activity is not needed in these countries. Watching briefs are appropriate where normal working relations with the Bank are disrupted by conflict, where the regular avenues for knowledge building have not been present in any formal and predictable way, or where a portfolio is inactive. In such countries a modest amount of Bank budget and staff time would be allocated to maintain a watching brief, and the guidelines for post-conflict reconstruction activities presented here would be applicable, at the appropriate time.

The Executive Directors would be informed when a watching brief is proposed. Where feasible, the Bank should work through resident missions or should form partnerships with agencies that have local representation. Coordination with the United Nations is critical. Regular consultation with international and local NGOs and other agencies—which, due to their activity in particular conflict situations, may have important data and experiences—is also important. These consultations do not take the place of interaction with established governments, but they do expand Bank understanding of a situation when other avenues of information are unavailable.

During the watching brief period, judgments about the opportunities and risks associated with a higher level of activity would be updated continuously. The Bank's recently created Post-Conflict Unit will, at the request of the responsible country managers, provide support and advice to design and implement watching briefs and facilitate cross-regional learning. Relevant country managers should provide to senior management with regular reports on the situation of watching brief countries that would include, among other things, key interactions with major donors, NGOs, and other agencies and a general overview of the situation, flagging important events or indications of potentially significant changes in the status of a country in question (for example, imminent peace negotiations). The views of concerned Executive Directors and key Bank staff responsible for operations in neighboring countries should be included in this process. In addition, the Post-Conflict Unit would prepare a brief annual report on the status of countries where watching briefs are in place.

Stage II: A Transitional Support Strategy

When it becomes clear that opportunities for useful intervention exist, the responsible Bank regional vice presidency would propose to the Bank's Operations Committee the preparation of a transitional support strategy. The proposal would give a general indication of the expanded requirements, in staff time and other resources, of the planning process, as well as relevant information regarding changes in a country's situation, the overall partnership strategy with the United Nations and other actors, and other issues. The approval of the strategy by the Operations Committee would trigger the initiation of activities outlined below. The Executive Directors would be consulted at this stage, presumably by an information note on which they may request a discussion.

In stage II, Bank staff would initiate a process of detailed assessment and planning that would, assuming no deterioration of the situation, culminate in a transitional support strategy. The Bank would also help prepare a national recovery plan in collaboration with the government and other major partners in reconstruction. This would be seen as the initial step toward a more comprehensive, full-scale reconstruction program. If conditions in the country do not allow Bank staff to travel there, alternative arrangements may be made, such as meeting with government officials outside the country or obtaining information from organizations within the country, including UN or bilateral agencies with relevant experience of the situation. At this stage the Bank may also provide critical advice on the economic impact of peace proposals. Allowance for this part of the Bank's work in post-conflict countries should be explicit in the administrative budget. During this phase, contingency plans for exit or for scaling-down of initiatives need to be developed by the country team. These plans would take into consideration such things as the likelihood of resurgence of violence, loss of international support, the type of intervention under consideration, and the risks.

Where the Bank has an active portfolio in a member country, the special budgetary provisions suggested for watching briefs are not required, even if the conflict is having significant impacts. As noted above, in such cases on-going project and sector work provides the knowledge of and contact with a country that are the objectives of a watching brief. In some instances, however, a borrower with an active portfolio may request the Bank's assistance in the reconstruction of conflict-affected areas of its territory. In such cases, and when in the judgment of the country manager special support is required, the preparation of a transitional support strategy would be warranted, as would the provisions (guidelines, risks, and so on) of all of the consequent phases of post-conflict assistance outlined below in regard to early reconstruction activities, post-conflict reconstruction, and so on.

The transitional support strategy presented to the Operations Committee would include a clear statement of risks, strategies for entry and exit, and the recommendations of regional management as to how the activities envisaged could be financed. Details of the strategy would vary depending on the country situation and the proposed program. Approval of a transitional support strategy would depend on fulfillment of three basic preconditions: sufficient indication that a sustainable cease-fire has been or will shortly be achieved; the presence of an effective counterpart for the Bank; and strong international cooperation, with a well-defined role for the Bank. The support of other donors could be gauged in relationship to resources mobilized. Upon the approval of the Operations Committee, the strategy would be submitted to the Executive Directors for their endorsement.

The transitional strategy submitted to the Executive Directors should include details as to how the overall proposal will be financed. Where possible, the proposed activities would be funded under normal Bank instruments. In some countries undisbursed amounts may still be available under existing loans or credits; or there may be alternative sources such as grants under the Institutional Development Fund (although these are limited in purpose and amount). In other instances, Social Funds represent useful instruments. If no sources are available quickly, either because of the time required to prepare a lending operation or because of nonmembership or nonaccrual status, the Bank would seek alternative funding mechanisms. In Bosnia and Herzegovina and the West Bank and Gaza, for example, special trust funds were established and allocations were made out of surplus. Where special funds are required to implement the transitional strategy, an accompanying recommendation would be made to the Executive Directors to this effect. Upon the endorsement of the strategy by the Executive Directors and approval of any special funding, early reconstruction stage would begin.[1]

Stage III: Early Reconstruction Activities

Rapid reaction to countries emerging from conflicts is critical to enable and reinforce an incipient peace process, deter a resurgence of violence, and build a foundation for longer-term reconstruction. Early reconstruction activities would be initiated as opportunities arise. They would be

---

Box 8 Early Reconstruction Activities

- Detailed project planning and preparation
- Urgent repair of vital facilities such as schools, health centers, sanitation infrastructure, and shelter, to benefit returning refugees and displaced people, as well as affected communities; construction of rudimentary communications and transport installations
- Pilot projects, to develop and test techniques for later expanded reconstruction
- Demining (immediate funding of demining institutions and demining of key infrastructure and refugee return areas; large-scale demining would likely take place later)
- Demobilization, including reintegration of ex-combatants (planning; preparation, such as needs assessment; and small-scale immediate demobilization activities, such as training and microfunding)
- Design of social safety nets in a post-conflict situation, taking into account changes in demographic and household structures—for example, a larger number of female-headed households—and dependency issues
- Small-scale and microenterprise credit schemes to restart production and promote employment
- Schemes to promote employment through infrastructure rehabilitation and small-scale construction or reconstruction ("social funds")
- Start-up and recurrent costs of an emerging administration (note that some recurrent costs—for police, for example—cannot be funded by the Bank)
- Technical assistance for restoring central and local government capacity
- Planning and implementation of programs to create the conditions for reintegration of populations displaced by the conflict.

---

[1] This funding may derive from many sources, including Trust Funds. If funding is allocated from Bank surplus or net income, approval of the Board of Governors will be required.

small-scale activities that can be undertaken relatively quickly—in many cases by or in partnership with UN agencies or NGOs—and would not be heavily dependent on normal Bank project preparation procedures. Small-scale activities during this phase, in addition to representing a response to the urgent needs of early transitions from conflict, can function as pilot activities that enhance learning for the design of later, larger-scale programs. Increased field presence is indicated during this stage to ensure that lessons developed in transitional activities are efficiently absorbed by the institution, to permit a rapid recognition of opportunities to move on to a further phase of activity, and to take note of warning signals that may indicate a deterioration of the situation requiring exit or a scaling-down of involvement.

Activities undertaken during this stage include planning and preparation for a large-scale reconstruction program to ensure an efficient and timely response when larger operations are possible. The type of activity would vary according to the circumstances in the country and may change over time as more experience is gained in post-conflict situations. During this early stage, however, activities are likely to include those noted in box 8.

As noted earlier, this initial operational involvement poses considerable risks. To mitigate these risks, the participation of all the parties to the conflict in the choices the Bank makes, as well as that of other international or nongovernmental agencies, may be necessary. The guidelines suggested below should help reduce some of these risks. The Bank should ensure that:

- The roles of various international agencies are understood and agreed upon.
- Active conflict has diminished to the point where Bank work can begin, and there should be a reasonable expectation of continued relative stability or of a sustainable formal cease-fire.
- The Bank has some presence on the ground and/or a satisfactory knowledge of the country, including an established dialogue with potential partners.
- The impact of the conflict on the economy, on communities, and on institutions makes immediate assistance necessary in order to develop an overall reconstruction program.
- The Executive Directors agree, in the case of nonmembers, that assistance is warranted "for the benefit of members." [2]

---

[2] Article III, Section 1(a) of the Bank's Articles of Agreement states, "The resources and the facilities of the Bank shall be used exclusively for the benefit of members with equitable consideration to projects for development and projects for reconstruction alike."

- There is an intention on the part of a nonmember country to become a member.
- There is a commitment by the civil authorities to work with the Bank on reconstruction and development issues.
- There is an administration in place that is capable of handling in-country implementation aspects of Bank-funded work, with selective support by organizations such as the UN system, the EU, bilateral agencies, or NGOs.

The Bank, in partnership with other donors, should be prepared to move incrementally during this stage; that is, where certain areas have become peaceful, and provided that other conditions are acceptable, the Bank should assist with reconstruction in those areas.

Stage IV: Post-Conflict Reconstruction

As soon as larger-scale operations are possible (that is, when peaceful conditions have persisted for some time, and there has been sufficient time for project preparation and for resolution of any membership or arrears questions), these operations should be carried out under either normal or emergency procedures, currently described in Bank OP/BP 8.50. These procedures will need to be interpreted flexibly and should be reviewed on the basis of experience to see if revisions are needed to respond to the particular needs and dynamics of post-conflict reconstruction. The kinds of activity undertaken will depend on the strategy worked out during the early reconstruction phase. For example, where security conditions and government commitment allow, broad support for reconstruction would include physical reconstruction, economic recovery, institution building, and social reintegration, including active participation of the communities themselves in design and implementation. In some countries, activities may address only certain regions where violence has abated. In all cases, programs designed for reconstruction cannot be implemented in isolation from other elements of a portfolio. The design and implementation of post-conflict reconstruction, even if focused on a particular region of a country, should, to the extent possible, integrate existing programs supported by the Bank. In essence, the Bank approach should be flexible and modular, modifying activities and adding on as conditions dictate. It is important to recognize that in many countries reconstruction programs have been put in place and are now in midstream.

Stage V: Return to Normal Operations

Throughout this process, but particularly when the emergency phase is over, operations are once more carried out under normal lending procedures, and the consciousness of conflict begins to wane, Country Assistance Strategies and economic and sector work should explicitly recognize the effects of the conflict and the sometimes permanent transformation of society that may make the return to the status quo ex ante impossible and even undesirable. The country assistance strategy and economic and sector work should spell out what is needed to ensure that future operations not only do not exacerbate existing tensions but also contribute in a positive way to growth with equity. Operations need to include social assessments that can address some of the fundamental issues related to the aftermath of conflict. As noted, this recommendation also applies to country assistance strategy work generally, particularly in countries viewed as "at risk."

Recommendations for Bank Operations

In addition to the organizing framework, this report makes several operational recommendations.

Field Presence

The Bank's responsibilities, and its core relations, are with its member states. For this reason, field presence is an essential part of the Bank's capacity to monitor, to maintain coordination with government and donors, and to respond flexibly to changes. Resident missions generally need to be strengthened to meet post-conflict roles, especially in maintaining partnerships and working on a day-to-day basis on project implementation with borrowers, UN agencies, and international and local NGOs. The devolution of authority to field managers in the West Bank and Gaza and in Bosnia and Herzegovina has proved critical for the success of these programs and should be considered for other countries where local dynamics are similarly complicated and in flux. Where a field office does not exist, one should be established, either in the country itself or, where this is not feasible because of security considerations, in a neighboring country.

Partnerships

The Bank needs to forge key partnerships with UN and other donor agencies as early as possible in conflict countries. International NGOs often play a crucial role in delivering services to populations in war-affected countries in which government capacity has been weakened or destroyed. The Bank can play an important role in supporting the transition from implementation by international NGOs to indigenous responsibility as a post-conflict government resumes its responsibilities. The presence of a large number of international NGOs often offers unique opportunities for capacity building during implementation, especially in the training of national staff. In a more general sense, the indigenous institutions of civil society (of which local NGOs form only a part) have a crucial role in restoring public confidence in peace and acting as bridges between different population groups and cultures.

Relief-Reconstruction Linkages

As a development agency, the Bank's main contribution in this area is likely to be in helping to close the gap between relief and development. Fostering a better understanding of the operational implications of the transition would help avoid negative patterns that can jeopardize later reconstruction and development activities. As reconstruction activities begin, wide-scale relief with large external funding needs to give way to well-targeted schemes to protect the most vulnerable. It is likely, however, that relief will continue to be needed during at least part of the reconstruction period. Relief programs need to maximize local input in order to build the capacity necessary for the early stages of reconstruction. The Bank should have a clear understanding, early in the process, of how its activities will affect and take over from emergency operations—for example, efficiently utilizing transitional food aid when necessary for development initiatives in accordance with new Bank policies. In Bosnia and Herzegovina the experience of the International Management Group (and, of course, cooperation with the World Health Organization, the Soros Foundation, and others) helped address some of the timing and resource gaps by compiling information early on. This kind of experience should be institutionalized in the forward planning carried out by the Bank and the international community.

Aid Coordination

Effective coordination requires both cooperation and leadership. It may not be possible to establish a model that will work in all situations, but a coordination plan for reconstruction efforts should be developed at a high level and should include a definition of the roles of the main players and which will provide the lead role in each sector. Coordination should not wait until program implementation but should begin with the earliest efforts at needs assessment and planning. The Bank, in partnership with other key donors, should be part of a rigorous management of the international community's role. Shared coherent policies on such issues as relief-reconstruction linkages and conditions for supporting recurrent costs should be included in the agreement.

The recent example of the interagency task force on Angola, appointed jointly by the heads of the World Bank, the IMF, and the United Nations, offers an interesting model of donor and agency coordination. For implementing programs, the use of a major trust fund, as in the West Bank and Gaza and in Bosnia and Herzegovina offers potential. It is recommended that in each post-conflict situation, international and bilateral agencies should agree on a blueprint for reconstruction, leadership, and delineated roles for various participants. The international response to conflict situations would be enhanced by a cohesive strategy for pooling donor resources. Reconstruction activities might ideally be financed out of a rapid-response trust fund, administered by the Bank itself or by any other multilateral agency, in which financial resources committed by the various donors are pooled. Expenditures might then be authorized in accordance with the previously agreed blueprint, and the administration would be fully accountable for the results on the ground and for financial probity. A common, unified set of simplified disbursement rules would be used, and there would be a time-bound termination of the fund.

New Operational Guidelines

The facility for emergency projects outlined in OP/BP 8.50 was designed to abbreviate approval procedures, largely to facilitate a rapid response to short-duration events such as natural disasters. Emergency lending procedures need to be specifically designed for the special circumstances of post-conflict countries—in particular, the diminished government capacity and the uncertain dynamics of reconciliation and unification. It is not feasible to anticipate all the scenarios for resolving the internal disputes that remain after cease-fire agreements have been reached. Assistance by the Bank and other donors needs to support this process, but patterns of behavior may be different from peacetime expectations. Guidelines may need to be amended or rewritten so that the Bank's response can follow a realistic appraisal of these dynamics and be tailored to the opportunities and constraints of individual situations. The guidelines could include streamlined procedures for procurement, audit, disbursement, and other matters, incorporating lessons from Bosnia and Herzegovina, Rwanda, and other post-conflict countries. The Bank's Operations Evaluation Department has undertaken a comprehensive study of the Bank's response to post-conflict situations around the globe. Following the completion of this study in the summer of 1998, the issue of developing new operational guidelines for post-conflict situations will be revisited and recommendations made for further actions.

New Areas of Operation

The new areas of activity described in "Adequacy of Existing Instruments" in chapter 2 require further support and development. The anticipated workload in demining might justify the creation of a panel of experts. Experience from the first projects will inform discussion on clearance standards, prioritization, and acceptable risk levels. The expertise on demobilization and reintegration of ex-combatants developed in the Africa region and described in a best practices paper (Colletta, Kostner, and Wiederhofer 1996b), is being drawn on elsewhere ad hoc, but current ability to respond is limited. Reintegration of displaced populations is clearly a major component of the reconstruction task, indicating a need for greater Bank expertise and capacity and for greater collaboration with the UNHCR. Sector work is needed, particularly where displacement is very high.

Flexible Funding for Early Reconstruction Activities

There is a clear need for flexibility and speed in assisting countries emerging from conflict, in the period before traditional lending can be made available. The commitment and delivery of early transitional funding from the Bank can be a vital confidence builder at a critical stage in post-conflict reconstruction. Early financing of Bank activities can be separated into two categories: financing of Bank administrative overheads and direct project costs. The issue of overheads is raised to some extent through discussion of the watching brief and in the assessment and planning phases of the Bank response. It should, however, be recognized that the overall budgetary requirements for operations in post-conflict countries are likely to be higher than in other countries. This lesson has been clearly learned during Bank operations in the West Bank and Gaza, Bosnia and Herzegovina, and other post-conflict situations. The situation in post-conflict countries is fluid and often volatile and requires careful and intensive monitoring by Bank staff. Operations in all sectors take on special significance when sustainable transitions out of periods of intrastate conflict are being supported, and they thus must be designed and implemented with extraordinary care. Nascent post-conflict government structures and fragile civil societies create conditions requiring extra attention by staff. The issue of funding for project costs during these phases has been addressed in the past on an ad hoc basis—for example through trust funds financed from surplus, as in the West Bank and Gaza and in Bosnia and Herzegovina, or through grants to UN agencies in the cases of Rwanda and Somalia. Partnerships with other donors and access to bilateral trust funds have also proved valuable in facilitating the financing of early project activities. The five-stage framework for post-conflict reconstruction outlined previously details the process whereby management will, in individual cases, make recommendations to the Executive Directors for special funding of such early transitional activities.

Bank Responsibilities for Post-Conflict Reconstruction

In order to manage the country risks inherent in post-conflict reconstruction, there is a need to know more about the dynamics and impacts of conflict and the relationship between development investment and conflict prevention and reconstruction. To maximize existing resources and manage the risks, it is recommended that the Bank rely primarily on a number of existing "pillars" at the country and regional level, with a small central focal point to marshal the best available knowledge, practice, and expertise.

Country Teams

Country teams are the first line in post-conflict activities. Weak or non-existent governments, the multiplicity of actors, political fragility, and the costs of missed opportunities all combine to suggest that more staff time needs to be allocated and a deeper understanding of social and political complexities needs to be developed. Bank operations are designed around active portfolios, and country departments may have more pressing tasks than groping for an understanding of the situation in countries whose emergence from conflict cannot be predicted. Country teams need to have assured resources for the watching brief, for planning and assessment, and for early stages of reconstruction. They also need to plan for a greatly expanded demand for staff and consultant resources for these countries.

Regional Teams

The impact of conflict is felt across national borders, and solutions often require the involvement of neighboring states. Regional multicountry investments or complementary programs in surrounding countries may be needed to ensure that peace and development are secured in the country emerging from conflict. The Bank is in a strong position to provide a regional response that includes partnerships with regional organizations. But the internal structure of the Bank, with its focus on individual countries, does not always allow meaningful subregional operations, particularly where regional departments separate neighboring countries, and additional attention is required to formulate operations involving several neighboring countries. The Africa region, which has several countries involved in post-conflict situations, has established a small team encompassing expertise in this area. There may be some justification for similar small teams in other regions, as conflicts may have particular regional aspects that can contribute to understanding of and assistance to reconstruction. Examples include, in Africa, the collapse of weak states and endemic poverty; in Europe and Central Asia, the transition from socialism to a market economy; and in Latin America and the Caribbean, the impacts of long guerrilla warfare. the decision to form such a regional post-conflict team should rest squarely with the regional management team.

The Bank's Post-Conflict Unit

The Bank recently established a Post-Conflict Unit (PCU), which became operational on July 1, 1997. The unit will act as a focal point for enhancing Bank response to the issues detailed in this report. The requirements of maintaining frequent contacts with other members of the international community, advising and briefing senior management on the Bank's activities in post-conflict countries, collecting information and monitoring developments in individual countries, developing and articulating policy options for the Bank in a continuously changing international environment, and guiding Bank staff on issues of common interest in this area are large and expanding. The previous arrangement of pulling in the limited available expertise to respond to each individual situation did not work satisfactorily. Many of the issues are central, and a core capacity is needed to consolidate learning; the Bank has not yet

fully understood the range of problems involved in rehabilitating societies that have so totally collapsed. The new central unit will initially
serve as a focal point for policy development, cross-country learning,
and development of expertise in specific skills for cross-support to regions. The Post-Conflict Unit is located in the Social Development Department of the World Bank, and its operations will be integrated closely
into the overall framework of social development within the institution.
The role of the post-conflict unit will be periodically evaluated.

To minimize the risk of the core unit's expanding its work beyond
requirements and, in particular, duplicating the roles established for UN
agencies and regional organizations, the terms of reference would limit
the group to the following functions:

- Providing a focal point for partnership with other members of the
  international community involved in post-conflict reconstruction,
  and helping Bank staff to benefit from the growing research on reconstruction both internally and in academic and policy institutions.
- Providing scarce specific expertise to the Bank's operational staff
  in areas such as demining, demobilization, and population reintegration.
- Maintaining a multisectoral expert capacity to back up country
  teams working on reconstruction issues. An appropriate skill mix
  will be achieved through a combination of permanent staff assigned
  to the unit, rosters of outside consultants, and identification of personnel in various regions of the Bank with special knowledge and
  experience to share with other country teams.
- Helping to organize missions to countries emerging from conflicts
  and participating in the design of reconstruction programs at the
  request of the regional offices. The unit will play a key role in supporting country teams in developing best practice in the implementation of watching briefs and will help to pilot the concept
- Accelerating the institutional learning process through analysis and
  dissemination of information on issues and practice. Activities in
  this category would include as managing a knowledge dissemination network (Web pages and other sources); maintaining a data
  base on issues related to post-conflict activities; bringing together
  staff from different regions to share lessons in reconstruction strategies; increasing staff awareness through contribution to training
  and Bank seminars; coordinating cross-country studies on new areas of activity such as land mine pollution, demobilization, refugee
  reintegration, and resolution of land tenure disputes; and developing best practices.

- Serving as the secretariat of the Bankwide group on post-conflict reconstruction issues.
- Monitoring and reporting to Bank senior management and the Executive Directors on progress in implementation of the Bank's policy and procedures; initiate changes in the policy whenever they become necessary in the light of lessons learned. In particular, the unit will prepare consolidated annual reports on cross-country experience throughout the Bank in the implementation of watching briefs.

Research, Evaluation, and Training

Evaluation of post-conflict reconstruction operations is essential for creation of a realistic analytical framework for policy development. Evaluation is needed to assess the impact of operations on recovery, identify best practices, evaluate the international coordination framework, and draw lessons for future operations. Evaluation case studies should be prepared as soon as there are lessons to be disseminated, without awaiting the completion report phase. To this end, it is suggested that the OED work with operating units to establish and improve monitoring and evaluation systems for the major ongoing programs such as that in the West Bank and Gaza. This process would strengthen accountability, provide comfort to the Bank's partners about the quality and rigor of Bank project monitoring and supervision, and document lessons learned. Joint evaluations with and by donors should be encouraged, where feasible, to conserve financial and administrative resources. Cooperation also seems desirable with the growing number of academic groups and think tanks attempting to come to grips with the problems of conflict and the transition to peace. The Bank's advisory services, including coordination, are of critical importance in reconstruction programs. They not only support the Bank's lending services but also establish the framework for post-conflict governments and the entire international response. There is potential for providing these services on a fee basis, on behalf of donors. The Bank's Economic Development Institute (EDI) is developing training courses on post-conflict topics such as reintegration, reconciliation, and economic recovery and is initiating country programs in Angola, Bosnia and Herzegovina, and the West Bank and Gaza. The Bank's Learning and Leadership Center is also expanding opportunities for Bank training in areas related to post-conflict reconstruction. *World Development Report 1997* (World Bank 1997), which focused on the role of the state in development, provided a forum for exploring impacts and patterns of state failure linked to conflict.

External Affairs

Conflict situations represent highly visible, volatile areas of work. The Bank should have a carefully articulated presentation of its activities in conflict countries. Since development assistance has not proved that it can provide comprehensive insurance against violent conflict, and since much remains to be learned about the science and art of reconstruction, the Bank should be careful not to present itself as a panacea for the international management of violent conflict.

Risks for the Bank

Bank operations in countries emerging from conflict are clearly not "business as usual." The Bank's involvement in such situations needs to be recognized as a specialized sphere of activity with its own mandate, distinct from but an essential first step toward, longer-term development, on a path that is unclear and uncertain. The risks for the Bank are fairly high, as the probability of reversals, setbacks, and failures is much higher than for normal operations. The nature, origin, and intensity of the risks for the Bank need to be fully recognized at the outset. First, there is a risk that Bank investments will not have the expected returns because of renewed hostilities or other political or military events or because of implementation difficulties stemming from weak institutional capacity, shortfalls in donor financing, or coordination problems. Second, there are risks to the Bank's reputation if stated objectives are not achieved because of the above events or if there were a perception of bias or inequities in the Bank's program that could jeopardize reconciliation objectives. Third is the security risk to Bank staff working in post-conflict countries.

Some of these risks can be mitigated by sharing the portfolio of activities with other bilateral and multilateral agencies, by building up better links with security and peacekeeping operations, by promoting improved methods of donor collaboration that include an agreed framework of actions, and by encouraging broader participation of all parties to the conflict, as well as other segments of civil society, in reconstruction work and thus raising their stakes in peace. Where these risks become unmanageable or cross the tolerance threshold, judgments have to be made by the managers concerned about the appropriate timing of postponement or cessation of Bank activities, as outlined below. The Board will be kept informed, at appropriate intervals, about the assessment of the risks and the steps being taken by management.

The post-conflict reconstruction work of the World Bank has to be firmly rooted in the Bank's mandate—to build a sustainable base for development. In a post-conflict situation, some prior activities that are taken for granted in normal borrowing countries may have to be supported. The restoration of normal living, working, and social conditions, the jump-starting of economic activities, the immediate rehabilitation of vital services such as water supply and sanitation and electricity, and help in getting key institutions into operation are some of the activities that distinguish borrowers in post-conflict situations from normal borrowers. Activities such as demining and reintegration of ex-combatants and displaced populations are also investments particular to post-conflict situations. Under no circumstances is it envisaged that the Bank will move into post-conflict countries unless other international actors are also involved. The Bank will play a complementary role to UN agencies and will step in, selectively, to help in areas in which it has a comparative advantage, such as physical reconstruction, institutional and social development, and donor coordination. It will focus on areas where other actors are not forthcoming and where the Bank's presence can leverage or open up other avenues of assistance and mobilize the resources of other agencies—bilateral, multilateral, or private. The Bank's graduated response will depend on the extent to which other actors get involved.

Annex A. Breaking the Cycle of Conflict and Resuming the Path of Development

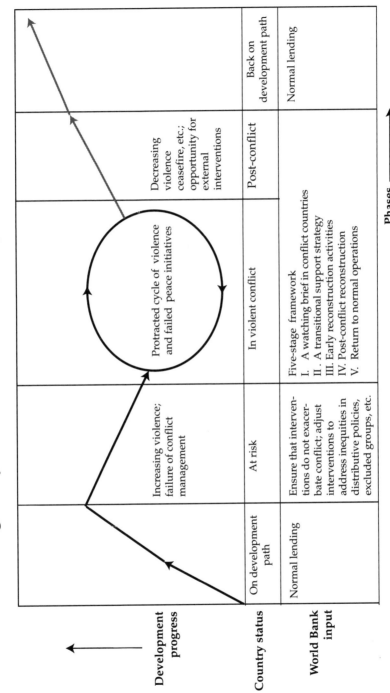

Development progress					
Country status	On development path	At risk	In violent conflict	Post-conflict	Back on development path
World Bank input	Normal lending	Ensure that interventions do not exacerbate conflict; adjust interventions to address inequities in distributive policies, excluded groups, etc.	Five-stage framework I. A watching brief in conflict countries II. A transitional support strategy III. Early reconstruction activities IV. Post-conflict reconstruction V. Return to normal operations		Normal lending

At risk: Increasing violence; failure of conflict management

In violent conflict: Protracted cycle of violence and failed peace initiatives

Post-conflict: Decreasing violence ceasefire, etc.; opportunity for external interventions

Phases ⟶

Annex B
External Roles in Conflict Countries

Actors	Political and diplomatic (conflict management, resolution, and avoidance)	Security (peacekeeping to prevent violence and enable relief and rehabilitation)
Donor states	Bilaterally and multilaterally (regional groupings such as the OSCE)	Peacekeeping forces
United Nations[a]	Security Council DPA/SRSG	DPKO/SRSG Peacekeeping forces
European Union	European Council European Commission European Parliament	Observers
NATO	Secretariat	Peacekeeping forces
NGOs	Human rights, conflict prevention	
IMF		
World Bank	Assessing economic impact of peace proposals	

Note: The divisions between relief, rehabilitation, and reconstruction is less clear in practice. Many agencies involved in emergency relief extend their programs into rehabilitation and reconstruction work. Development agencies may identify opportunities for appropriate interventions in some instances or in specific sectors even during what is notionally viewed as an "emergency relief" or "conflict " phase.

[a] Description of UN agencies: within the UN family, security issues are mainly the concern of the Department of Political Affairs (DPA) and the Department of Peace-Keeping Operations (DPKO). Other agencies such as the UNHCR, UNICEF, and the WFP, play critical roles in relief and in activities necessary in the transition from relief to development. The UNDP is increasingly involved in post-conflict reconstruction activities, as are the Food and Agriculture Organization of the United Nations (FAO) and the World Health Organization (WHO). Various initiatives are un-

Emergency relief (basic needs; maintenance of human and social capital)	Reconstruction (rebuilding physical and economic assets, restoring institutional capacity, etc.)
Mainly through agents (UN, ECHO, NGOs); some use of military	Bilaterally and through agents
Through UN agencies (OCHA, WFP, UNHCR, UNICEF, others)	UN agencies (UNDP, UNHCR, UNICEF, OCHA, OPS)
ECHO (also through UN agencies and NGOs)	European Commission (DGs I and VIII), UN agencies (UNDP, UNHCR, UNICEF, OCHA) NGOs
Independent/as agents of governments/UN/EU	Independent or as agents
	Macroeconomic assistance
No relief, but increased role in monitoring during conflict and in providing nonlending services	Flexible range of lending and nonlending services working toward normalization

der way to improve coordination both within and among UN agencies. The Office of the Coordinator for Humanitarian Affairs (OCHA) has developed its role at three levels: between departments such as the DPA and the DPKO in the UN secretariat; between other UN organizations such as the UNDP, the UNHCR, the WFP, and UNICEF; and with the ICRC, NGOs, and other bodies through various cooperative networks. Much of its coordination work has focused on information sharing and the preparation of consolidated appeals. The OCHA has also sought to facilitate the transition to developmental activities, and in some conflicts it has extended its role into in-country operational coordination. The UN Secretary General recently initiated a system-wide process of developing a "strategic framework" for coordination of all United Nations activities in post-conflict situations. SRSG is the Special Representative of the Secretary General. OPS is the UN Office for Project Services.

Annex C
World Bank Operational Guidelines for Financing Land Mine Clearance

1.   A number of member countries have recently asked the Bank to consider financing land mine clearance. Dealing with demining presents many delicate issues for the Bank, but it is clear that once hostilities have ceased and peace has been restored in a project area, removal of land mines may be essential to reestablishing normal development activities and undertaking productive investment. Financing land mine clearance is similar in many ways to financing other types of land preparation for development activities (clearing stumps for cultivation or landslides on roads); however, because of the particular political and safety factors generally associated with demining, requests to finance such activities merit special attention and approaches. This memorandum sets out guidelines for staff to follow in considering such requests.

Eligibility

2.   To be eligible for Bank financing, land mine clearance must be an integral part of a development project or a prelude to a future development project or program to be adopted by the borrower. The Bank may support land mine clearance to make available land and infrastructure that are required for a development activity agreed with the borrower. It is this development activity that the Bank seeks to support, rather than land mine clearance per se. This development activity should be identified no later than at the appraisal stage of the land mine clearance and should be documented, even though it may be financed by the Bank or other sources at a later stage.

3.   The following are examples of the types of land-mine-related activities for which the Bank may provide financing in the context of a project.

   (a)   *Capacity building*: support for the development of national or local demining centers to create or expand capacity to implement the demining components of projects in priority sectors (transport, agriculture, reintegration of displaced people and refugees, etc.). Such centers typically include facilities for lodging, training, and equipping deminers; capacity for mine-awareness training; and a mine information center that conducts mine surveys and disseminates updated information on the status of mine clearance in specific targeted areas. The Bank's Institutional Development Fund may finance the setting up of the institutional capacity and the training of personnel in demining.

(b)   *Area demining programs*: financing of a demining program in particular areas of a country as a component or first phase of a development project or program that aims to (i) reintegrate displaced populations and reactivate the local economy, and (ii) carry out additional development activities (repatriation assistance to refugees, Quick Impact Projects to rehabilitate agriculture, reconstruction of health and education facilities, etc.) that may be funded by the Bank, UNHCR, UNICEF, or other agencies.

(c)   *Sector demining programs*: support for demining programs targeted at specific sectors; for example, demining of agricultural land as part of a larger agricultural rehabilitation program or demining of roads and bridges as part of a transport project.

Economic Justification

4.   The financing of land mine clearance activities must be justified on economic grounds and must take into account the scarcity of financial resources.

Implementation Responsibility

5.   Land mine clearance in Bank-financed projects must be carried out under the responsibility of civilian authorities. However, this requirement does not preclude collaboration with the military (for example, on maps, surveys, removal of mines) and the employment of former military personnel.

6.   *Borrower.* The borrower and the implementing agencies are responsible for evaluating alternative land mine removal methods,

choosing among them, and implementing the chosen method. The Bank requires that the borrower obtain competent independent technical, financial, and legal advice on all aspects of project design and implementation; and it may require that the borrower establish a panel of internationally recognized experts to advise on the project.

7.   *Bank staff.* Bank staff make clear to the borrower and implementing agencies that the Bank does not have institutional capability in the technical aspects of demining, including assessing risks associated with alternative technical approaches, and that the borrower and implementing agencies should not act in sole reliance on any views that Bank staff may express in this respect. Bank staff should exercise utmost caution in discussing technical aspects with the borrower and implementing agencies. Bank staff include in the project documents a brief summary of the process by which the borrower and implementing agencies have made the technical choices and a description of the quality assurance process to be put in place.

8.   *Consultation with UN Agencies.* As appropriate, Bank staff consult with relevant UN agencies (DPKO/UNMAS, OCHA, UNHCR, UNDP, etc.) or the ICRC to avoid duplication of efforts and to obtain the benefit of their technical expertise. Similarly, staff are encouraged to exchange views with NGOs and other bilateral agencies, as appropriate.

Procurement

9.   Land mine removal is a difficult and dangerous task, and even experienced professional disposal teams cannot be sure that they have located and cleared all mines from the land. Even a 99 percent rate of successful clearance in a field seeded with 1,000 mines leaves 10 unexploded mines. The cost of insurance to the contractor could be high. Justifiable insurance costs may be included in the project cost.

10.   Bank procurement arrangements are based on considerations of economy and efficiency. At the same time, in view of the high risk and limited sources of expertise involved in land mine clearance, procurement arrangements for these projects, including bid documents and contracts for land mine removal, must be tailored to the needs of the specific project. Contracting arrangements need to ensure that risks are appropriately identified and allocated and that any insurance arrangements are adequately reflected. All procurement and contracting arrangements must be cleared by the Procurement Policy Adviser, OPRPR.

Conditionality, Board Presentation, and Supervision

11.   The legal agreements for any project involving land mine clearance include a covenant under which the government undertakes not to lay new land mines anywhere in the country that would in any way undermine the execution or development objectives of the project.

12.   When the loan is presented to the Board for approval, regional staff indicate to the Board whether and to what extent the country has renounced the use of land mines. If, during project implementation, the Bank receives evidence of new mine-laying activity in the country, the regional vice president notifies the Board of the event and any effects it may have on the project.

Annex D
World Bank Operational Policy on Emergency Recovery Assistance (OP 8.50)

1.   A country may request assistance from the Bank[1] when it is struck by an emergency[2] that seriously dislocates its economy[3] and calls for a quick response from the government and the Bank.

2.   The main objectives of emergency recovery assistance are to restore assets and production levels in the disrupted economy. The Bank finances investment and productive activities, rather than relief[4] or consumption, and focuses on areas of its comparative advantage. Immediate relief activities are best carried out by local groups, the government concerned, bilateral relief programs, nongovernmental organizations (NGOs), and specialized international relief organizations.

Forms of Bank Emergency Assistance

3.   Bank emergency assistance may take the form of (a) immediate support in assessing the emergency's impact and developing a recovery strategy; (b) restructuring of the Bank's existing portfolio for the country, to support recovery activities; (c) redesign of projects not yet approved, to include recovery activities; and (d) provision of an emergency recovery loan (ERL).

Emergency Recovery Loans

4.   ERLs are designed to help rebuild physical assets and restore economic and social activities after emergencies. ERL activities address restoration of assets and production, rather than relief. An ERL takes into

---

Note: The policies set out in OP 8.50 apply to all projects for which the first mission begins after September 1, 1995. OP, BP, and GP 8.50 together replace OD 8.50, Emergency Recovery Assistance, and draw on the Operational Memorandum Disclosure of Factual Technical Documents, 6/20/94. Questions may be addressed to the operations advisers, Operations Policy Group, OPR.

account the Country Assistance Strategy and sectoral development strategies. The country lending program may be adjusted to accommodate a new ERL, normally within the country's general lending allocation.

Criteria

5.   The Bank considers the following criteria in deciding whether to provide an ERL: (a) impact on economic priorities and investment programs; (b) frequency (for recurring events, such as annual flooding, a regular investment loan is more appropriate); (c) urgency (for a slow-onset disaster such as a drought, the more thorough preparation of a regular investment project may be preferable); (d) prospects for reducing hazards from similar natural disasters in the future; and (e) expected economic benefits.

Design Considerations

6.   Normally, an ERL is fully implemented in two to three years. Each ERL project is adapted in form and scope to the emergency's particular circumstances and retains flexibility. ERL projects use disaster-resilient reconstruction standards. They also include emergency-preparedness studies and technical assistance on prevention and mitigation measures to strengthen the country's resilience to natural hazards or lessen their impact.

Conditionality

7.   ERLs do not attempt to address long-term economic, sectoral, or institutional problems and do not include conditionality linked to macroeconomic policies. They include only conditions directly related to the emergency recovery activities and to preparedness/mitigation in the event the disaster recurs.

Procurement, Disbursement, and Retroactive Financing

8.   Standard Bank operational policies, including those on procurement,[5] consultants,[6] and disbursement,[7] apply to ERLs. ERLs may include quick-disbursing components. However, a distinction is maintained between ERLs and adjustment lending: an ERL is designed to finance only a positive list of imports identified as necessary to a well-defined recovery program. Disbursements can be made for up to 100

percent of the imports' cost. No more than 20 percent of loan proceeds may be used for retroactive financing of expenditures, and the payments must have been made after the emergency occurred and within four months prior to the expected date of loan signing.[8] In exceptional circumstances, with the approval of the managing director, operations, concerned the date of the first mission or the date of the emergency event may be used as the earliest date for expenditures eligible for retroactive financing.

Donor Coordination, Local NGOs

9.   When designing quick-disbursing components under ERLs, the Bank coordinates with the IMF regarding the country's plans to use the Fund's Compensatory Financing Facility for recovery activities. Collaboration with the United Nations Development Programme and other international agencies, local NGOs, and donors is often helpful in devising the recovery assistance strategy under an ERL and in designing specific prevention and mitigation programs.

Prevention and Mitigation Projects

10.   In addition to emergency assistance, the Bank may support free-standing investment projects for prevention and mitigation in countries prone to specific types of emergencies. Such operations could assist in (a) developing a national strategy, (b) establishing an adequate institutional and regulatory framework, (c) carrying out studies of vulnerability and risk assessment, (d) reinforcing vulnerable structures and adjusting building and zoning codes, and (e) acquiring hazard-reduction technology.

---

[1] "Bank" includes IDA, and "loans" includes credits.
[2] For the purposes of this statement, an emergency is an extraordinary event of limited duration, such as a war, civil disturbance, or natural disaster. Examples of natural disasters include cyclones, droughts, earthquakes, floods, forest fires, and tidal waves.
[3] Serious economic dislocation caused by external economic shocks or other situations justifying adjustment lending is not considered an emergency.
[4] Examples of relief activities include search/rescue, evacuation, food/water distribution, temporary sanitation and health care, temporary shelter, and restoration of access to transport.
[5] See OD 11.00, "Procurement," and *Guidelines: Procurement under IBRD Loans and IDA Credits* (Washington, D.C.: World Bank, 1995).
[6] See OD 11.10, Use of Consultants," and BP 11.10, Annexes D and D1.
[7] See OP/BP 12.00, "Disbursement."
[8] See OP and GP 12.10, "Retroactive Financing;" and OP 12.10, "Retroactive Financing: Amendment to the Processing of Exceptions" (memo from Jan Wijnand, OPR, to senior operations advisers, 2/8/95).

Selected Bibliography

Ball, Nicole. 1996. *Making Peace Work: The Role of the International Development Community.* Washington, D.C.: Overseas Development Council.

Colletta, Nat J., Marcus Kostner, and Ingo Wiederhofer, with the assistance of Emilio Mondo, Taimi Sitari, and Tadesse A. Woldu. 1996a. *Case Studies in War-to-Peace Transition. The Demobilization and Reintegration of Ex-Combatants in Ethiopia, Namibia, and Uganda.* World Bank Discussion Paper 331. Washington, D.C.

————. 1996b. *The Transition from War to Peace in Sub-Saharan Africa.* Directions in Development series. Washington, D.C.: World Bank.

Holtzman, Steven. 1995. "Post-Conflict Reconstruction." Work in Progress Paper. World Bank, Environment Department, Washington, D.C.

Kumar, Krishna. 1996. *Rebuilding Societies after Civil War.* Boulder, Colo.: Lynne Rienner.

Muscat, Robert. 1995. "Conflict and Reconstruction: Roles for the World Bank." World Bank, OED, Washington, D.C.

IMF (International Monetary Fund). 1996. *A Macroeconomic Framework for Assistance to Post-Conflict Countries.* Paper for OECD/DAC Task Force on Conflict, Peace and Development Co-operation. Washington, D.C.

Steering Committee of the Joint Evaluation of Emergency Assistance to Rwanda. 1996. *The International Response to Conflict and Genocide: Lessons from the Rwanda Experience.* Copenhagen: Danish International Development Agency (DANIDA); London: Overseas Development Institute.

UNDP (United Nations Development Programme). 1996. *Building Bridges between Relief and Development.* A Compendium of the UNDP Record in Crisis Countries. New York.

World Bank. 1995. "The World Bank's Role in Conflict Prevention and Post-Conflict Reconstruction: A Staff Perspective on Operational Issues and Constraints." (Groupware Sessions). Washington, D.C.

————. 1997. *World Development Report 1997: The State in a Changing World.* New York: Oxford University Press.